Management Face-to-Face

Management Face-to-Face

Derek Torrington
Professor of Human Resource Management, UMIST

Prentice Hall
New York · London · Toronto · Sydney · Tokyo · Singapore

First published 1991 by
Prentice Hall International (UK) Ltd
66 Wood Lane End, Hemel Hempstead
Hertfordshire HP2 4RG
A division of
Simon & Schuster International Group

© Prentice Hall International (UK) Ltd, 1991

Typeset in 10/12 pt Palatino
by Pentacor PLC, High Wycombe, Bucks

Printed and bound in Great Britain by
BPCC Wheatons Ltd, Exeter

Library of Congress Cataloging-in-Publication Data

Torrington, Derek, 1931–
  Management: face to face / Derek Torrington.
    p. cm.
  Rev. and expanded ed. of: Face to face. 1972.
  Includes bibliographical references and index.
  ISBN 0–13–543422–X
    1. Employment interviewing.   2. Negotiation in business.
3. Employee counseling.   4. Public speaking.   I. Torrington, Derek,
1931–   Face to face.   II. Title.
HF5549.5.C6T65   1991   90–20452
658.3'145—dc20   CIP

British Library Cataloguing in Publication Data

Torrington, Derek 1931–
  Management face to face.
  1. Managers. Interpersonal relationships with personnel
  I. Title
  658.315

    ISBN 0–13–543422–X

---

3 4 5 95 94 93 92

Contents

Preface

This book is part of a twenty-year obsession with the idea that what really makes managers effective is their ability to deal with people face-to-face.

In 1972 I published a slim volume entitled *Face to Face*, which set out a model for managers of four interactive encounters: selection, counselling, negotiation and addressing an audience. Each was presented in a simple sequence of preparation, encounter and follow-up. This has been a satisfactory book, remaining in print for ten years and selling in different parts of the world.

In 1982 *Face-to-Face in Management* extended the original face-to-face idea to eight different encounters, with the addition of more detailed general material at the beginning. Although it did not sell as widely as the 1972 volume, it was again a very satisfying book to write. Now the management-competences initiative brings a third version. Although a reluctant convert to the idea of management competences (and even more reluctant about competencies), I remain convinced of the need for management competence.

There has been some extensive reworking of the early chapters and modification of the remainder, as well as adding in the encounters of selling and appraisal, making a total of ten. The final chapter is now devoted to three types of group situation.

I am indebted to my friend and colleague Jane Weightman for reading the manuscript and making many suggestions for improvement, as well as keeping an eagle eye on the 'hes' and 'hims'. I have tried hard to remove the implications that all managers are male, but I am afraid I can still not bring myself to describe a chairman as a piece of furniture. As ever, I appreciate the skill and guidance of the Prencice Hall professionals, especially Cathy Peck, my editor, and Nick Waller, who provided the illustrations. Most of all I acknowledge the assistance of hundreds of managers and management students who have helped, usually unwittingly, to shape the material during the last twenty years.

situations. These will mainly be aspects of understanding other people and getting messages across to others. Secondly, there is a discussion of typical face-to-face situations, with suggested ways of handling them.

The management process

The nature of management work shows a change of emphasis. The traditional focus on decision-making is now shifting towards decision implementation. John Harvey-Jones of ICI used the phrase 'making things happen', which neatly expresses the change. Some decisions are obvious, some are inescapable, some are so complex that only a computer program can make them, but only skilful humans can make things happen.

This increasingly requires managers to involve non-managerial employees in the decision implementation, as they can no longer depend on the straight-forward exercise of authority or power. As the jobs to be done in organizations become more skilled, managers become more dependent on the skill and training of many different people to understand the varied organizational requirements that the manager is trying to co-ordinate.

An example is the work of the account director in an advertising agency, where the copywriter, the artist, the photographer and others all have to be brought to share the same vision of what they are together going to produce. The contribution that each can make has to be understood by the account director and the vision of what is possible from the group will develop through the consultative process.

With the increasing complexity and specialization of organizational tasks, employee contribution can rarely be commanded in the sense that a manager knows what is to be done, the employee does not; the manager gives instructions, the employee complies precisely and then waits for further orders. Sometimes the contribution can be specified by a manager deploying an employee with known expertise who is required to use skill and knowledge to achieve a stated objective ('repair that machine' or 'check this building for fire hazards'). But typically in the 1990s the contribution has to be devised while it is explained, interpreted, justified, modified and delivered as the manager constantly blends the work of various people in getting decisions made and implemented.

Review topic 1.1

Think of a management decision in your recent experience that had to be altered or abandoned because it was clearly 'wrong'.

1. Was this because the decision was basically unsound or because it was not properly implemented?
2. How could the problem have been avoided?

The professional manager, task forces and networks

Managers need to operate as members of many different working groups or task teams. For the team leader, and the team members, this presents the need to adjust their social style constantly to a fresh group of semi-strangers. They all have autonomous expertise, but it is only their collaborative efforts that will bring achievement. This mixture of autonomy and interdependence has to be orchestrated by the manager.

At the same time managers are becoming slightly more professional in the sense of being self-reliant and independent. There is less tight, formal interdependence of people in clear hierarchical relationships and more flexible forms of organization with a strong emphasis on managers developing and maintaining extensive networks of personal contacts. John Kotter (1982) has described networks as a reflection of the political activity of managers. The individual manager identifies a large number of people, both inside the organization and outside, who will help in getting things done by providing information, speeding something up, cutting through some red tape, altering a priority, chasing progress, checking data, endorsing a proposal in committee, arranging for the manager to meet someone and doing jobs.

Networks are personal rather than hierarchical, although position in the hierarchy is crucial to having a good network as all network relationships are reciprocal, but expertise and social skilfulness are also important. People respond to requests not just because they 'owe you one', but because they respect you, can understand what you want, believe it to be legitimate and worthwhile, and because they like the contact with you.

There is also some move towards professionalising the work of interpersonal communication in a different way. The semi-permanent selection interviewer has been a feature of organizational life for many years, but more recently we have seen the appointment of professional counsellors, negotiators and change agents, as well as consultants on virtually every topic known to man. We have market-research interviewers, trade instructors and lecturers; and the twin activities of management development and performance appraisal enable some people to make an art out of assessment interviewing.

Professionalizing a job always produces a range of insider techniques to justify the profession. It is declared as being special and sufficiently unique for people to do nothing else. In that case there has to be a magic component to justify the specialization. This is usually some esoteric knowledge or developed skill. Professionalizing interaction has specialized the skills of interaction. The selector specializes in selection and the negotiator specializes in negotiation: simple fluency or 'being good at communication' is no longer enough for the specialist, although each manager has to maintain a general level of competence in all areas.

Customer care and competitiveness

The most marked change in orientation in business activities during the 1980s was towards looking after the customer. Expensive programmes of training were undertaken to turn the attention of people in organizations away from preoccupation with internal organizational politics and towards the customer, making them more responsive to those whose reponse was crucial.

Some results of this have been pointless, like the man leaning on a trolley at the railway station who had a standard response of 'Dunno, mate,' to anyone who asked the time of any train going anywhere. He still leans on the trolley but answers, 'I regret, Sir, I do not have that information.' Other results have been quaint, like the train guard who delivered short lectures over the public address system on local history of the towns the train was passing. The general effect, however, has been to increase considerably responsiveness to other people. Social-skill training begins with developing the self-confidence of the person under training and then sensitivity to the feelings and responses of others. Only at the end of the training is there a treatment of techniques, such as saying 'How may I help you?' instead of 'Next please.'

Growing understanding of face-to-face encounters

We come to know more about interactions almost daily, as various studies are published. Unfortunately, more knowledge does not always mean better understanding, as the studies tend to diverge rather than converge, but here are some of the areas of explanation.

Sensitivity training is a technique which develops the awareness that participants have of themselves, their effects on other people and the ways in which small groups operate. The method is to bring together a group of 7–10 people without any leadership or agenda and ask them to discuss what is happening to them. The lack of direction makes them dependent on their own resources in a novel way as they lack the support of any behavioural norms or cues. The effect is to strip away the veneer of conventional social behaviour, gradually revealing the true self and feelings that are conventionally masked. This reveals starkly how one is perceived by others and can develop forms of interaction that are more sensitive to the reactions of others and therefore develop greater interpersonal effectiveness.

A follow-on is the work of the American psychiatrist Eric Berne, who analysed relationships between people as game-playing and then evolved a form of therapy he called transactional analysis. This has subsequently been adopted as a means of developing an effective interpersonal style.

Social anthropologists aid our understanding of interaction by explaining the importance of ritual. Once we begin to appreciate the place of ritual in social life, then we understand those aspects of behaviour which otherwise appear irrational and obstructive. When aspirants for professional/managerial/administrative posts attend selection interviews they present themselves in a stylized way: 'well-washed and quietly-dressed . . . politely attentive, submissive, and keen . . .. He may need to show what a decisive and forceful person he is – but without using those powers on the selection board'. (Argyle, 1972, pp. 201–2).

This is not because all those who sit on selection panels believe it important to be able to wear a pin-stripe suit, but because there is an appropriate ritual for the employment interview and the applicant who broke from the ritual behaviour would feel insecure. One anthropologist has claimed:

> Rituals reveal values at their deepest level . . . men express in ritual
> what moves them most, and since the form of expression is
> conventionalised and obligatory, it is the values of the group that

are revealed. I see in the study of rituals the key to an understanding of the essential constitution of human societies. (Wilson, 1954, quoted in Sutherland, 1978, p. 44)

If ritual is a profound aspect of our behaviour, we cannot dismiss it, as so many managers do, as being 'mere' ritual that should be ignored or eliminated in order to get on with what really matters. Hundreds of elements in interactions exist primarily or partially for ritualistic reasons, and these are as important to effectiveness as any other aspect.

Erving Goffman (1969) offers an analysis of interaction in terms of the performances that people present to others. He argues that all of us are constantly seeking information from each other that is not readily revealed, so that we infer it from a range of cues, like gesture. At the same time we are deceiving those trying to obtain the same sort of information from us by the art of impression management, through which we try to create impressions of ourselves that are more favourable than the facts warrant. He also describes the way in which behaviour alters between what he calls the 'front' regions of workplaces and 'backstage'. Just as actors present one sort of performance on the stage and behave quite differently as soon as they are out of public view, so Goffman describes exactly the same behaviour by all people at work. Negotiators manage the impression they are creating while negotiations are in progress, but as soon as there is an adjournment the impression management is relaxed and exchanges are more informal and revealing of true feelings.

A surprising influence on interaction has come from the more popular aspects of the work of a series of zoologists (some better described as ethologists) who have come to conclusions about human behaviour as a result of studying the animal world and then making the logical step that man is an animal and therefore similar. Lorenz (1966) and Ardrey (1969) produced explanations of aggression and territorial protection that were to prove influential on popular opinion, and helped to modify folklore in organizations about the effect, for instance, of the interviewer's desk on the attitude of an interviewee. More recently, Desmond Morris has produced a series of books stripping away some of the concealing layers of human behaviour to reveal the 'naked ape' beneath. His most important work in the context of interaction is a natural history of gestures (Morris, 1977a and Morris et al. 1977b) that complements the work of psychologists studying non-verbal behaviour.

Review topic 1.2.

Replay in your mind a recent important meeting with one other person and identify aspects of ritual and the use of gestures to communicate.

Effectiveness in interaction

How do you succeed? How do you become a good communicator? It is not easy, firstly because few people can face up to the fact that they are not already good communicators, as it seems such a fundamental aspect of being a member of the human race. Secondly, our interactive behaviours are so deeply ingrained and well practised that they cannot readily be altered.

With the growing understanding of the interaction processes, it is, however, possible to develop greater competence. It is important to fit competence to situations: for example, an effective selection interviewer may be a poor negotiator, and many effective trainers could not sell ice cream to eskimos. The bulk of this book contains action guides to different situations, but there are still some general factors that can make one person more effective than another.

Poise enables a person to be at ease in a wide variety of social situations, often enjoying them, and able to talk with different types of people in a relaxed and self-confident way. This self-confidence derives partly from the feedback of willing responses constantly provided by other people.

Another element of poise is knowing what you are talking about; so we demonstrate our poise much more in situations with which we are familiar than we do in strange circumstances. There is less fear of what others may say and less apprehension about appearing naïve. Questions, and even criticism, are easier to deal with and are often wanted, so stimulating the interchange.

Poise is often associated with maturity, due to a person having succeeded in developing a rounded view of themselves without too much anxiety about the possible adverse opinions of others. This can be accelerated by experience which involves meeting a variety of people from differing backgrounds.

A necessary adjunct to poise is the quality of being responsive to the needs, feelings and level of understanding in other people. This prevents poise from becoming too egocentric. The teacher, for instance, will be looking for signs of misunderstanding in the student so that the message can be restated or clarified, and the market-research interviewer will be looking for signals that the question has been accurately construed, or that it needs elaboration.

At another level there will be responsiveness to the emotional state of the other. The training of dentists used to include 'watching the dial', observing the face of the patient while drilling holes in their teeth. When the patient winced, the dentist would ease the drill away from the nerve that was being macerated. Other people at work do not usually inflict physical pain in quite the same way, but they will be on the look-out for signs of physical discomfort in those with whom they are speaking. 'Can you hear?', 'Can you see?', 'Are you in a draught?', 'Is the sun in your eyes?' are all questions to which answers will be sought, even though the answer may be inferred by some aspect of the other's behaviour rather than as a spoken response to a spoken question.

Responsiveness can also include offering rewards, like friendliness, warmth, sympathy and helpfulness, as features of general style or as part of a relationship with other participants. These not only sustain and strengthen the relationship, they may also be held back as a means of manipulation in trying to get one's own way.

Much of human artistry in performance depends on timing. This is most obvious in the physical arts like dance, gymnastics and ball games, but is also a requirement of any vocal performance. The operatic duet, the cross-talk comedy act or any stage play, all depend upon the skill with which the performers time their exchanges. The exchanges which are the subject of this book also depend on timing, without the complication of an audience as a third party. Skill is required first in adapting to the speech of others and then taking control to move into a smooth pattern of exchanges. The other person may be bright or dull, bombastic or diffident. The skilled interactor uses poise and responsiveness to 'pick up' the rhythm of the other and either adjusts to that or adjusts both rhythms to provide the basis for comfortable exchanges. A helpful analogy is learning to play tennis, where the tyro is absolutely dependent on the person at the other side of the net. The skilled player will help the learner by playing back the ball in a way that the learner can cope with and gradually sharpens the game by speeding up the exchanges.

Timing difficulties occur when one party tries to override or interrupt the other because of impatience, or where there are misunderstandings and awkward silences in the exchange. They can also be caused by lack of social skill or by a phase in the interaction which presents particular problems or anxieties to one of the parties.

Often the context of the exchange is the overriding consideration. If you have to tell someone that they are to be dismissed, the style and the context of the exchange will both be important. If you have to tell someone that they have passed their examinations, the gladness of the tidings makes the subtleties of interaction irrelevant. This is complicated by the expectations we all have. The opening gambit of, 'Come in and sit down, John. There is something I want to talk to you about', tends to signal bad news, and if you have bad news to deliver it is most infuriating when you signal it in behaviour and then laboriously prepare the ground in what you say before you deliver the message.

David Penny was made redundant after thirty-one years service as a technician. He recalls the Monday morning when the technical director came up to him in the laboratory with the question: 'Oh, David, have you got a minute? There's something I want a word with you about. Let's go into this office here.' He was then told that he was being made redundant, that there was no need to stay any later that day and if he would just sign the form to acknowledge receipt of the cheque, he might as well be getting off. 'It's a nice day, why not have a round of golf?'

Recollection has doubtless modified some details of that exchange, but the place of the conversation, the perfunctory nature of the information and the crassness of the suggestion about the round of golf are absolutely reliable. We would all agree that it was handled badly, yet this type of hamfistedness is an everyday occurrence.

Problems in interaction

There are certain general problems that impair effectiveness. They are mostly ways in which people tend to hear what they expect to hear.

The frame of reference is the standpoint from which a person views an issue, and understanding of the issue will be shaped by that perspective rather than any abstract 'reality'. A purchase is, for instance, seen quite differently according to whether you are buying or selling. It is not, however, simply a question of the role that is being played in the situation. The frame of reference is a set of basic assumptions or standards that frame our behaviour. These assumptions are developed through childhood conditioning, through social background, education and affiliations, and differences in the frames of reference held by participants in interaction present inescapable problems. Can the Russians and the Americans ever really understand each other? How can those who manage and direct ever appreciate the point of view of those who are managed and directed?

The frame of reference on any particular matter is largely determined by opinions developed within a group with which we identify, as few of us alter our opinions alone. We both follow and participate in the formulation of opinion in our group, and most of us are in a number of such reference groups. This produces complexities: some people can be vociferously anti-union as citizens and voters in general elections, yet support a union of which they are members at their workplace.

A manager who is trying to persuade someone to change their behaviour or attitude to work may have to struggle with the fact that the values informing the behaviour of that person are different from their own, may not alter, or may move only when the values of their reference group alter. Both participants in the interaction will 'see reason', but the reason they see will be different.

The stereotype is the standardized expectation we have of those who have certain dominant characteristics: all Scots are mean; all shop stewards are disruptive; all mathematicians are poor in using words. The behaviour of some people in a category makes us expect all in that category to behave in the same way (Figure 1.1). This is obviously invalid, but it is a tendency to which we are prone so that we are likely to hear someone say what we expect them to say rather than what they do say.

Figure 1.1 *Stereotyping*

At first this is necessary in working relationships; it is not feasible to deal with every individual we meet as being a void until we have collected enough information to know how to treat them, so we always try to find a pigeon-hole in which to put someone. We begin conversations with a working stereotype, so that we stop someone in the street to ask directions only after we have selected a person who looks intelligent and sympathetic. If we are giving directions to a stranger we begin our explanation having made an assessment of their ability to understand quickly, or their need for a more detailed, painstaking explanation. The stereotype becomes a handicap only when we remain insensitive to new information enabling us to make a rational appraisal of the individual with whom we are interacting.

Being aware of the dangers of stereotyping others, and trying to exercise self-discipline, can reduce the degree to which you misunderstand other people, but you still have the problem that your respondents will put you into a stereotype and hear what you say in accordance with whatever that predetermined notion may be.

Cognitive dissonance is the difficulty we all have in coping with behaviour that is not consistent with our beliefs. This will make us uncomfortable and we will try to cope with the dissonance in various ways in order to reduce the discomfort. Either we persuade ourselves that we believe in what we are doing, or we avoid the necessary behaviour. When we are given new information that is not consistent with what we already believe, we are likely to massage it to fit our existing pattern of behaviour rather than jettison the beliefs of a lifetime.

It was explained very carefully to Fred Longworth that it was no longer necessary for him to keep detailed ledger records, as the computer would do that for him; all he had to do was to make the decisions. Fred nodded eagerly, for we seldom acknowledge that there is a dissonance in our cognitions; but three weeks later the night watchman came across him at three in the morning secretly bringing his ledger up to date (Figure 1.2). Cognitive dissonance makes it hard for us to understand new information, harder to believe in it and hardest of all to take any action based upon it.

Table 1.1 *How do you communicate?*

In conversation I concentrate on making what I say as clear as possible: if I can understand it, anyone can.

In conversation I am always keen to listen to what the other person is saying and make my contribution fit.

Managers must concentrate on making the best possible decisions, regardless of potential problems of putting them into practice.

Decision-making is easy. A manager must concentrate on making the decisions work and changing them when they won't.

If I have a job to do then I am responsible for results.

I'm just one of a team. We all share all the praise and all the blame.

The organization chart tells me where I stand and where I go for decisions and action.

I know a lot of people and rely on them to help me in all sorts of ways to get things done.

I am very sensitive to the opinions of other people and always anxious to be 'in their good books'.

If there is a right way to do things, that's how I like to do them.

I find most people interesting and always welcome meeting new faces.

If you want to get a point across to someone, you have to start from where they are.

I like the easy to-and-fro of conversation.

I never worry too much about what other people think of me.

Petty social conventions irritate me. I like to get on with things.

I get on well with people of the same background and interest as myself.

I will always find time to explain things to people who are genuinely interested.

In conversation I often find I can't get a word in unless I interrupt. Some people simply won't listen.

Review topic 1.3

1. Think of a friend, colleague or relative and write down three differences between their frames of reference and yours. To what extent do these differences complement each other to make for effectiveness and to what extent do they create misunderstanding and reduce effectiveness.
2. Write down (for your eyes only) five stereotypes in your mind which influence the way you deal with certain types of people. Do you find these rough-and-ready guides useful? How often are you wrong?
3. Identify a change in working practices which you resisted because of cognitive dissonance. How do you feel about it now?
4. Can you overcome these problems of inadequate understanding of other people without becoming characterless? Is there a danger of being bland without integrity?

Figure 1.2 *Fred Longworth could not believe, but would not say . . . .*

The importance of interaction lies in its function of making things happen in organizational life. However detailed the application form and however elaborate the tests, it is the interview which determines whether a potential employee joins the organization or not. Getting the purchase correctly specified, appraising performance, negotiating contracts, training, negotiating agreements, selling products, terminating contracts and so on all depend on discussion. These relatively formal exchanges are in addition to the thousands of minute-by-minute conversations that encourage, reassure, explain, advise, rebuke and inform.

References

Ardrey, R. (1969) *The Territorial Imperative*, Collins, London.

Argyle, M. (1972) *The Psychology of Interpersonal Behaviour*, Penguin, London.

Berne, E. (1966) *Games People Play: Psychology of human relationships*, Andre Deutsch, London.

Berne, E. (1972) *What Do You Say After You Say Hello?*, Andre Deutsch, London.

Goffman, E. (1969) *The Presentation of Self in Everyday Life*, Penguin, London.

Harvey-Jones, J. (1988) *Making it Happen: Reflections on leadership*, Collins, London.

Kotter, J. (1982) *The General Managers*, The Free Press, New York.

Lorenz, K. (1966) *On Aggression*, Methuen, London.

Mintzberg, H. (1973) *The Nature of Managerial Work*, Harper & Row, New York.

Morris, D. (1977a) *Manwatching*, Jonathan Cape, London.

Morris, D., P. Collett, P. Marsh, and M. O'Shaughnessy (1977b) *Gesture Maps*, Cape, London.

Sutherland, A. (1978) *Face Values*, BBC Publications, London.

Exercise 1

There is no model communicator; no single style that leads to success. All of us can, however, do a little better by identifying small points for development. This short exercise is designed to start you reflecting on how you communicate. You pick out some of the features of your approach that you might be able to alter slightly, while remaining comfortable.

1. Each pair of boxes in Table 1.1 contains contrasted statements referring to an aspect of managing face-to-face situations that has been referred to in this chapter. For each pair put a tick somewhere on the connecting line to show where you think you are in relation to the two extremes.

2. Think of someone of similar position and temperament to yourself, who you think is generally better than you are in face-to-face situations. Repeat the first part of the exercise, using crosses instead of ticks on Table 1.1. to locate them between the extremes.

3. What does the comparison suggest to you about how you could improve your performance?

4. Select one of your ticks and try to move it during the next week.

5. At the end of the week, reflect on your experience. What have you learned? What have you changed? Are you going to try and move another tick?

6. Are you in danger of becoming a chameleon, or like an actor playing a part?

This exercise should not be taken too seriously. It is simply to start you thinking. The comparison (2, above) is to help you understand how *you* perform and should not lead you to copy that person slavishly, or you will become the chameleon mentioned here.

2 Without a word being spoken: Reading the non-verbal signals

In every conversation you have, only a small proportion of the understanding you develop comes from the words you hear. Researchers have made estimates, varying from 7 to 35 per cent, of the impact that words make in communication (Mehrabian, 1972), the remainder coming from the body language or non-verbal communication of facial expression, gesture, posture and other signals. A useful illustration is to watch any film made by a gifted director, where long passages are carried through without any dialogue, the story being told visually.

In many situations verbal and non-verbal communication are combined, like banging on the table to emphasize a point in argument or beckoning at the same time as saying, 'Come here', but each method is best for conveying certain types of message. Words are best for providing factual information, like someone's name, the price of a product or the essence of the company's mission statement, but non-verbal signals are the most effective and convincing for conveying feelings and attitudes. The laborious routines of sign language, semaphore or morse are a poor substitute for the easy precision of spoken words, and the subtle differences between fine wines are inadequately defined by the esoteric jargon of connoisseurs using such phrases as 'smoky dry', 'flowery fragrant when young, but with sharper overtones when older', 'long nose' and 'full-bodied'.

An important difference is that words are inert, so that you cannot know whether or not they are true: only the behaviour of the speaker shows the truth of the message. In every conversation the other person is lying to you. The lies are usually white lies, but they still obscure the truth. Often it is in minor, unimportant ways. If someone says, 'Hello, how are you today', the reply will usually be along the lines of, 'Fine, thanks. How are you?', no matter what the true state of mind or health that the other is experiencing, although the tone of voice or facial expression may send a quite different message. We make varying degrees of effort to appear interested when cornered by a bore: only an extraordinary person would use words such as, 'No, I do not wish to talk with you because you are boring', but we may well send that message with our accompanying behaviour, like the furrowed brow, the obvious looking at the watch or the sudden response to an imaginary wave from someone at the other end of the corridor.

Sometimes the lie can be important. Trainees may say they understand when in fact they do not, believing that misunderstanding will make them foolish or get them into trouble. The candidate in a selection interview will frequently be less than candid for fear of losing the job offer. In a number of situations managers are told by employees what they 'want' to hear rather than what they need to hear. Man is a dissembler. This is both a feature of manners, that require us to refrain from certain types of frankness, and an aspect of how we manipulate situations or manage the impressions we convey to others. There is always the temptation to find out what the other person is really thinking by getting behind the words and seeing the 'truth' in involuntary gestures, signs and cues that signal an attitude or an emotional condition that is contradicted by accompanying words. In a David Lodge novel, managing director Vic Savage is trying to find out whether or not he is being undercut by a competitor. He visits his customer, who assures him it is true, but is it? After the conversation his companion tackles him:

> 'He didn't tell you who the other company were.'
> 'I didn't expect him to. I just wanted to see his expression when I asked him.'
> 'And what did it tell you?'
> 'He's not bluffing. There really is someone offering four or five per cent below our price.' (Lodge, 1988, p. 143)

All of us do this, and most of us think we are pretty good at it, relying on intuition and experience. It can, however, be a dangerous temptation as the evidence that can be gained from these non-verbal cues is unreliable. Folding arms does not always indicate aggression and soft, wet, flabby handshakes do not invariably mean that the other person is of low moral fibre.

Even though prediction is unreliable, a study of non-verbal behaviour can give us additional inklings of what other people might mean and feel. This understanding can also help us in the way we convey meaning to others.

How understanding of non-verbal communication has developed

Understanding others by looking at them is an art with a long history of folklore and half truths. Consider how Hamlet interpreted a simple picture of his father:

> See what grace was seated on this brow;
> Hyperion's curls; the front of Jove himself;
> An eye like Mars, to threaten and command;
> A station like the herald Mercury
> New lighted on a heaven-kissing hill –
> A combination and a form indeed
> Where every god did seem to set his seal,
> To give the world assurance of a man.

> (Act IV, scene 2)

Apart from the general impression that is conveyed, is there a sort of eye that can threaten and command, so that when you see it you know how to respond? It is a superb image, but of doubtful practical value. Equally dubious are ideas like the weak chin, the strong face, the stiff upper lip and other sayings attributing an aspect of character to a physical feature.

An early attempt to make sense of the signals was the invention of physiognomy – judging character from facial features – by Aristotle. He observed that each animal has a special predominant instinct, so that the fox is cunning and the wolf ferocious. He then argued that men with features resembling a particular animal would have qualities similar to that animal. The idea fascinated the French and German painters Lebrun and Tischbein in the seventeenth and eighteenth centuries before finding its best-known advocate in Johannes Lavater. In 1775 he published a four-volume work setting out a system for reading the character in a face from its lines and contours. Although he became a celebrity and gained enthusiastic adherents as diverse as Goethe and Catherine the Great, his system was not soundly based, so that physiognomy now has no more credibility than phrenology or palmistry. Its weakness is demonstrated by the fact that Lavater describes a profile that almost exactly duplicates his own as: 'The countenance of the hero: active, removed both from hasty rashness and cold delay. Born to govern. May be cruel but scarcely can remain unnoticed' (Good, 1976, p. 23). We will still see sensitive faces, soulful eyes and determined chins, but we can only make these judgements erratically and on the basis of personal experience.

The first systematic investigation of non-verbal communication was in the work by Charles Darwin, *The Expression of the Emotions in Man and Animals*, which was published in 1872. The search for explanations in the behaviour of animals and man is also a feature of the recent past, with a number of people studying and reflecting upon behaviour in its natural state. The leading contemporary exponent of this form of analysis is Morris (1977, 1979) although earlier writing by Lorenz (1952, 1966) and Ardrey (1969) provide insights that are particularly relevant to instinctive behaviour.

Different from the natural-history approach is that of the psychologist, whose recent contributions have been through controlled experiment and the testing of hypotheses. Founding father, Sigmund Freud, made the comment in 1905: 'no mortal can keep a secret. If his lips are silent he chatters with his finger tips, betrayal oozes out of him at every pore.'

The greatest degree of uncertainty in interpreting the behaviour and intention of others by looking at them is the effect of culture. There is, for instance, marked variation in the degree of physical contact that is made in different societies. The European visitor to the Middle East is surprised to see young men walking along the street hand-in-hand. Leaders of the USSR greet visiting dignitaries by kissing on both cheeks: behaviour most unlikely in their American counterparts.

Ekman, Ellsworth and Friesen (1971) tested the universality of facial-expression meanings by showing photographs of university students to aborigines and asking for judgements about the feelings that were being expressed. The aborigines then posed for photographs that were shown to American students. Although the two sets of judgements were not perfect, there was a high degree of correlation, suggesting that the following emotions produce facial expressions that are universally recognizable: anger, disgust, fear, interest, joy, sadness, surprise.

The researchers also observed that it was much more difficult for someone to judge the intensity of emotion in a person of a different culture. It is easy to tell that they are angry, but how angry? This element of universality is not surprising when we appreciate that some components of facial expression are very difficult to control, like perspiring, blushing and trembling. Other ways we reveal our feelings are easier to control and therefore more variable from one culture to another. The work of Desmond Morris has been largely concerned with this type of variation in gesture, for example:

there is a simple gesture in which the forefinger taps the side of the nose. In England most people interpret this as meaning secrecy or conspiracy . . . 'Keep it dark, don't spread it around,' but as one moves down across Europe to Central Italy, the dominant meaning changes to become a helpful warning: 'Take care, there is danger – they are crafty.' The two messages are related, because they are both concerned with cunning. In England it is we who are cunning, by not divulging our secret. But in Central Italy it is they who are cunning, and we must be warned against them. (Morris, 1977, p. 53)

Interest in reading non-verbal behaviour is universal and is a crucial aspect of all face-to-face encounters at work. Some people reach a high degree of skill through experience and sensitivity. The remainder of this chapter provides a basis for being more skilful than those who rely solely on experience. What can we learn of the ways in which the feelings and intentions of others can be inferred from an aspect of their behaviour? How can we control our own non-verbal behaviour to fit our objectives in talking with other people?

The use of space

The anthropologist Hall (1959) coined the word *proxemics* to describe the way in which space is used as a form of communication. Basically, we move closer towards those we like and trust, but away from those we fear or dislike. Hall identified four zones around each individual (Figure 2.1):

- *Intimate zone* (0–0.5 metre). This is only viable when there is an intimate relationship with the other person or when the two are fighting. Touch and smell are important means of communication, as it is difficult to see clearly. Words can be whispered.

- *Personal zone* (0.5–1.5 metres). The two people must be well acquainted to feel comfortable, although they do not have to be intimate. Conversation is likely to be hushed.

- *Social zone* (1.5–3.5 metres). This is the zone in which most business behaviour takes place, as befits the impersonal relationship between, say, salesmen and client.

- *Public zone* (3.5 metres +). At this range strangers do not exist as individuals and can be comfortably ignored. If there is to be interaction words have to be delivered loudly, as on public occasions.

This tendency to move closer to those we like or in whom we have confidence, and to move away from those we fear or distrust explains

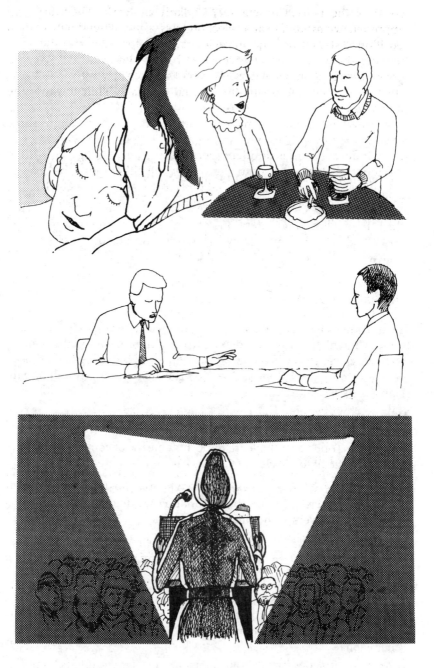

Figure 2.1 *Individual zones of communication*

some of the behaviour we see regularly at work. The wary and apprehensive candidate at a selection interview will tend to take up a position distant from the interviewer, perhaps even unthinkingly moving the chair slightly backwards before sitting down. If confidence develops in the interview and the way in which it is being conducted, then the orientation would gradually shift towards the interviewer.

A powerful senior manager, wanting to work through some documentation with an assistant, may say 'Pull up a chair and look at this.' If the assistant is diffident (perhaps as a result of having written the report that is being scrutinized) they will either move the chair to a relatively distant position so that it is only possible to see by leaning forward uncomfortably and unnaturally, or will leave the chair where it is and go to stand by the senior manager, leaving the comfortably distant chair to retreat to at the earliest possible opportunity. Actually pulling up the chair in the way suggested would be too close for comfort.

Space also involves territory. One reason why the assistant does not want to get too close to the superior is because the superior's desk and chair have territorial-defensive indicators all over them to assert ownership. There are the studio photographs of the children, the personalized key-ring attached to the key in the lock of the private drawer, the desk set, the blotter with doodlings in the top right-hand corner, the glasses, the tooled leather diary with gold-embossed initials, the stainless steel paper knife and all the paraphernalia that says to other people: 'This is mine; keep off' (Figure 2.2).

There are all manner of ways in which this territory is protected and used in organizational life. Open-plan offices are full of rubber plants and filing cabinets that are gradually shifted, nudged and rearranged until each occupant of the office has marked out their own territory and put small walls round it. Waiting rooms and lifts provide daily examples of territory definition. The first person in the waiting room will take up the best strategic position – back to the wall, able to see the door, not likely to be overlooked. The next best position is logically the adjoining chair, but that is one place that will not be occupied by the next person to come into the room.

When people enter a lift there is a clear sequence. The first person takes up a position just inside the door, near the controls. The second person goes to the diametrically opposite corner. A third will stand in one of the two remaining corners, and numbers one and two will both squeeze themselves more firmly into the corners they have already occupied. Number four takes up the last corner and number five has no choice but to stand, vulnerable, in the middle. As more

Figure 2.2 *Establishing territorial defences*

enter there are desperate attempts by everyone to avoid touching if possible and all eyes are fixed intently on the indicator of which floor the lift has reached. Nobody speaks and all seem almost to be holding their breath until the doors open and someone gets out to relieve the tension.

Scheflen (1972) gives useful advice on how to select conversations to break in on at receptions and buffets. If two people are talking while facing each other directly, they would not welcome interruption; if they are at an angle of 90 degrees to each other they are probably hoping to be interrupted, and if the angle is any greater they are pleading for help!

This is echoed in the conclusions of Sommer (1969) and Cook (1970), both of whom demonstrated a relationship between positioning around tables and the nature of the interaction (Figure 2.3). Those preparing to compete, negotiate or argue sat at opposite sides of a table, while those expecting to co-operate were more likely to sit side by side. The preferred position for conversation was for the parties to sit at a 90 degree angle.

Morris describes how territory can be protected in a public library. A pile of books on a table effectively reserved the chair adjacent to the books for 77 minutes, and a jacket over the back of the chair extended the reservation period to 120 minutes (Morris, 1977, p. 132).

Figure 2.3 *The relationship between positioning around a table and the nature of interaction*

The value of understanding some of these signals is to be able both to identify them and manipulate the situations in which they occur. If a factory manager is about to conduct some negotiations with a group of shop stewards it would not be helpful to arrange the furniture as if for a friendly, brainstorming type of meeting. The negotiating nature of the encounter is best reflected in opposed, 'them and us' seating arrangements. A counselling interview will involve building a degree of mutual confidence that may be difficult to achieve across a desk, but much helped by a 90 degree orientation.

The observant selection interviewer will not produce questions that might sound threatening until the applicant begins giving some of the small signals that indicate growing trust and confidence: various aspects of the applicant's posture will move towards the interviewer rather than pulling back.

Review topic 2.1

Consider how the furniture is organized in your office. It is probably arranged to make efficient use of space and light. Are there any changes you can make to make your meetings with people more effective?

Posture

Most people realize that they show their feelings in their faces, but few know that they also do this in their posture, so there is less likelihood that posture will be controlled to prevent the observer picking up any clues. For this reason it can be a useful source of information. In an argument, for instance, someone may unwittingly signal defeat by allowing their shoulders to slump while continuing to be defiant in their language.

Height is a significant aspect of posture (Figure 2.4). Tallness tends to make one person physically dominate another and relative shortness is seen as a disadvantage for which the short seek compensation by aggressiveness, volubility or some other dominant characteristic. Women are normally shorter than men and have been wearing much higher heels for a very long time to even up that difference. Public speakers stand on a rostrum or in a pulpit. We look up to our idols and look down on the worthless.

In organizational life we emphasize or underplay our height according to the situation. A foreman feeling the need to assert

Figure 2.4 *Height is a significant aspect of posture*

himself with a member of the department will tend to pull his head up and back in order to 'look down' on the subordinate. The salesman leaving a meeting with a client who is likely to place an order will tend to duck his head as he leaves and bow slightly when shaking hands in an instinctive display of deference to the person whose goodwill must be maintained. The 'honorific behaviour' of the Japanese is one of the most extreme forms of manipulating relative height, with their deep, long bows. Similar is the 'wai' in Thailand, where the hands are placed together in greeting, but then raised above the eyes during a courteous, small bow.

Mehrabian (1972) has explained some posturing according to what he calls the 'immediacy principle', similar to the proximity principle already mentioned. Immediacy behaviours are leaning forward, touching, getting close and looking straight at the other person (Figure 2.5). All these improve mutual visibility and reduce the distance between the two people, so that some of these behaviours will be displayed by the person who is drawn to, confident in or friendly towards the other. If our feelings about the interaction are negative, then we will tend to pull back, lean back, turn our head away, break eye contact and depart as soon as possible.

An interesting feature of posturing is what has been called the

Figure 2.5 *Immediacy behaviour*

postural echo, or <u>mirroring</u>, whereby one person automatically adopts the general posture of the other, or adopts one particular feature of that collection of postures (Figure 2.6). If someone is telling a story to a friend, the listener (once interested) is likely to pick up and unknowingly mirror an aspect of the story-teller's posture – hand to chin, legs crossed, leaning forward, leaning backward or some similar echo of the other's posture.

In organizational life it is possible to use an understanding of this to manipulate interactions. A personnel officer who has to conduct a disciplinary interview which involves trying to understand why an employee is not acquiring the necessary degree of speed and accuracy on an initial training programme, may find that the trainee comes and sits quietly, hands on lap, looking at the floor. If the personnel officer then also sits down quietly and mirrors the other postural components <u>there will be a quicker and more meaningful response</u> than if the personnel officer stands at the window with arms folded.

Another example is judging the mood of a meeting, where two contrasted points of view are being expressed. <u>The non-committed will gradually mirror the postures of those whose point of view they find most persuasive. Also their posture may change as their mind changes, so that they signal a growing uncertainty by dropping a postural echo.</u> The highly observant group leader can thus decide the

Figure 2.6 *Postural echo or mirroring. One person adopts the general posture of another*

appropriate time to take a vote or to express a view that should gain general consent.

Posture change is also used in a more deliberate, knowing way to send messages. In the next chapter we have a note on how to close interviews, including the use of postural signals, but at this point think of how you use posture to discourage casual visitors and to get rid of people who have overstayed their welcome.

Monica had almost finished drafting her report when Nigel barged into her office. She kept her eyes averted, hunched her shoulders in concentration, swivelled her chair slightly away from Nigel and said in clipped tones to the window opposite the door through which he had come, 'Nigel, I'm trying to finish this report.' Nigel left. He then barged in on Sally next door, who had also almost finished drafting her report. She too said, 'Nigel, I'm trying to finish this report,' but at the same time she turned to look at him, smiled in a long-suffering sort of way, relaxed in her chair and put her pen down. Nigel stayed (Figure 2.7).

Figure 2.7 *Different reactions to Nigel*

Review topic 2.2

Make a list of posture signals you use to discourage people; not gaze, words or gestures, just posture. Think of a few more you could add to your list and then try them out, singly and in combination. Then do the same thing for posture signals to encourage people.

Gesture

Some gestures are obvious and universal in their meaning. Beckoning, for example, means the same thing wherever it is used (Figure 2.8). General emphasis, or underlining, is found extensively in gesture, and the meaning is again unequivocal – banging on the table or other behaviour that accompanies and directly relates to what is being said.

Hewes (1973) has suggested that gesture preceded language as a means of communication among primitive people and that we retain the remains of a gesture language to accompany our speech, so that we are able to make ourselves understood with relative ease on most

Figure 2.8 *Some gestures are obvious and universal in their meaning*

matters when among foreigners with whom we have no common language. It is also interesting that more gestures are used in the conversation of those with high verbal facility than by those without, so that gesture supplements speech rather than substitutes for it.

Because of the connection between gesture and language there is also a strong connection between gesture and culture, so that it seems quaint to Western eyes when a Russian leader responds to applause from his followers by clapping himself.

Gesture is used to synchronize verbal exchanges. This is mainly done by language and gaze, but is supported by gesture. If you are in conversation with someone who you realize is about to speak, but you have not yet completed your point, you will not only talk louder and more quickly, you will probably also look directly at the other person, raising your eyebrows and producing a blocking gesture towards the other person by raising your hand, with the palm down. If, on the other hand, you reach a point where you want to signal the other person in, then your voice will soften, get slower, your expression will become open and the accompanying gesture will be more relaxed and with the palm up (Figure 2.9).

Figure 2.9 *Using gestures to synchronize verbal messages*

Gestures that reveal something about a person involuntarily are difficult to decode. Shivering can indicate either cold or nervousness because both trigger the central nervous system to produce the same physical result. Rubbing palms indicates anticipation, while rubbing the back of one's hands indicates cold. Shrugging shoulders shows disinterest and waving means 'good-bye'. Much less obvious and well known are the more obscure displacement activities that have been identified by physiologists. When in a state of stress we sometimes engage in behaviour which is irrelevant or out of context. The prospective father waiting anxiously for his wife to produce their first child in the next room typically walks up and down to relieve the tension. In other situations people scratch their heads when baffled, and a typical gesture – particularly in women – in reacting to news of a crisis is to clasp the forehead (Figure 2.10).

Krout (1954) conducted a series of experiments to identify what he called autistic gestures, that were involuntary indicators of specific attitudes (Figure 2.11). Among his less obvious conclusions were the following:

- steepled fingers indicate suspicion.
- hand to nose indicates fear.
- fingers to lips indicate shame.
- open hand dangling between the legs indicates frustration.

Figure 2.10 *Some people scratch their heads when baffled,*
or react to news of a crisis by clutching their brow

Gaze

As with gesture, gaze is a component of synchronizing in interaction,
so that we look at the other person twice as much while they are
talking than while they are listening to us. In talking we look away
more in order both to collect our thoughts and to spare the other
person the uncomfortable experience of being looked at while
inactive. If we are wanting to signal the other into the conversation
('Nearly finished what I'm saying; your turn coming up') we will
wind up our contribution by accompanying our closing words with a
period of looking at the other directly, with slightly raised eyebrows.
The exchange of looks forms a strong bond between people. The
waiter in the restaurant may ignore you for a long period, but once
you have 'caught his eye' he is drawn towards you, however
reluctantly.

Important managers arriving in the office are at pains to acknowledge everyone they pass on the way to their sanctum. A nod, a half-
smile, an eyebrow flash; whatever the signal, it is accompanied by a
brief instant of eye contact to recognize and acknowledge. The

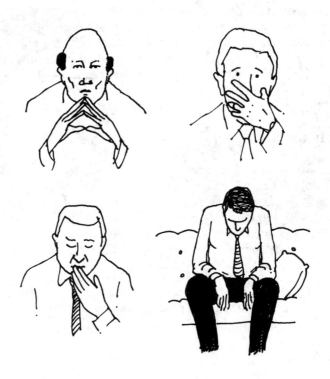

Figure 2.11 *Krout's autistic gestures*

manager who does not do that but marches purposefully in, looking neither to the right nor the left, sends shock waves rapidly round the building.

Generally the direction of gaze is a device for keeping the other 'in play'. Public speakers will sweep their eyes round the audience from time to time to maintain the bond. If they fail to do this and fix their eyes on their notes or a corner of the ceiling, then the audience will tend to lose concentration. In a different way the same principle applies in one-to-one encounters. The counsellor looks at the client to signal attention and understanding, and to provide feedback, otherwise the client will talk with less precision. If the counsellor looks at the client too much or too intently, the client will be inhibited.

Forbes and Jackson (1980) showed that gaze is one of the more telling aspects of non-verbal behaviour for applicants in selection interviews. They studied various aspects of the ways in which school-leavers behaved in applications for apprenticeships. Those applicants who produced more smiling, eye contact, head nodding and head shaking than average improved their chances of being offered a job. Variations in body position were not found to have any effect on selectors' decisions. The behaviours which produced the favourable effect on interviewers were, of course, all ways of showing interest.

Bodily contact

A very specialized method of communicating is by physical contact. A pat on the back is both physically and metaphorically a way of encouraging. Less common in business life are spanking and stroking, although their verbal equivalents are extensively used. The great message-sender is the handshake. Folklore decrees that a firm, dry handshake comes from someone with a strong character and reliable personality, while a limp, moist handshake comes from someone who is weak and untrustworthy. Although this is obviously misleading, as anyone can produce a firm, dry handshake if they think about it, conventional wisdom still says that character can be judged from this momentary contact; partly because this is the only exchange of this type that we ever have.

There are handshake variations that can be deployed to indicate greater degrees of warmth and reassurance, or dominance. The first is to hold on for a longer period. If that is accompanied by a vigorous pumping action it conveys enthusiasm for the meeting. The other main variant is the use of the left hand. This may be added to the basic hand-to-hand clasp, or may take hold of the other's forearm, elbow or shoulder. All of these convey friendliness, plus an edge of superiority and initiative-taking in the relationship.

A variant that is becoming more common is the forearm nudge or 'jollying', where someone reinforces the immediate bond between themselves and another by a nudge or brief grip on the forearm.

Miscellaneous aspects of non-verbal behaviour

The way we dress and groom our personal appearance contains a set of signals about how we want to be appraised by others, particularly the social grouping with which we identify. There are a number of uniforms for different occupational groups; the clearest examples being barristers, who always wear formal black suits with a white shirt or blouse. Sales representatives have a norm of charcoal grey suiting, white shirt or blouse and executive brief case.

Novices usually adopt the uniform of their occupational group willingly, as it provides them with a sense of security that comes from being clearly identified with those already established. As the sense of occupational security increases, so the grooming becomes more personal and idiosyncratic. Potter (1970, p. 177), provides a nice satirical comment on professional uniforms by showing the Hampshire general practitioner in top hat and frock coat while the president of the Royal College of Physicians wears an old fishing jacket.

Frequently, people in conversation use artifacts as ways of gaining time for thought. Most common are pipes and spectacles. If the pipe smoker is asked a question and wants to take time to reply without giving the impression that he needs time, he may relight his pipe or plunge a dead match into one of its noisome recesses for a second or two. The spectacle wearer may put them on to look at something, or may suddenly realize that they have been mislaid, so that a short space of time can be won by busily patting pockets and peering myopically under pieces of paper scattered about the desk. Other ploys are fishing a handkerchief out from pocket or handbag, being overtaken by a slight fit of coughing, or simply moving from one position in the chair to another. Bolton (1987, p. 83) describes the man who, when he wanted to terminate a conversation, 'made a desperate-looking grab for the cigarettes in his left-hand coat pocket'.

Quite the most puzzling aspect of body language is the difference between the sexes and the way in which certain conditioned interpretations of behaviour are related to gender. Traditionally, it has been an advantage to a man to be tall and many behaviours are linked to making the most of that. Women are rarely as tall as the men they are speaking with, so they have tended not to develop the same postural variations. The folklore decreeing that handshakes should be firm and dry is a folklore for men. Until recently it was unusual for women to shake hands at all, so there is fortunately no folklore of stereotyped assumptions about what a woman's handshake 'means'.

There are physical differences between men and women, but there are further differences that are socially constructed. Both are real, but those in the second category are changing. The difficulty is to know the speed of change.

Although sex differences in human performance are amenable to careful study from a variety of perspectives, one of the most striking considerations relating to this topic in everyday life is the extent to which specific beliefs about such differences are widely shared even though they cannot be substantiated by scientific research. (Durkin, 1987, p. 142)

Finally, the importance of non-verbal behaviour is demonstrated by the fact that it is more cogent than speech. Actions literally speak louder than words, and when they conflict the action wins. A popular party game for children involves a leader giving instructions, with gestures, for the children to follow. Occasionally the instruction and the accompanying gesture conflict and all those who followed the gesture rather than the words drop out. This game will usually last for five or ten minutes. If the rules are reversed so that players drop out when they obey the gesture rather than the words, there is such a low failure rate that the game lasts twice as long! The interviewer who signals inattention or impatience by shuffling papers and drumming fingers on the table will find that this signal overrides any words such as, 'Now how can I help you?'

References

Ardrey, R. (1969) *The Territorial Imperative*, Collins, London.

Bolton, R. (1987) *People Skills*, Simon & Schuster, Brookvale, New South Wales.

Cook, M.(1970) 'Experiments in orientation and proxemics', *Human Relations*, 23, 61–76.

Durkin, K. (1987) 'Social cognition and social context in the construction of sex differences', in M.A. Baker (ed.), *Sex Differences in Human Performance*, John Wiley, Chichester.

Ekman, P., P. Ellsworth, and W. V. Friesen (1971) *Emotion in the Human Face: Guidelines for research and integration of the findings*, Pergamon Press, New York.

Forbes, R. J. and P. R. Jackson (1980) 'Non-verbal behaviour and the outcome of selection interviews', *Journal of Occupational Psychology*, 53, 65–71.

Good, P. (1976) *Human Behaviour: The individual*, Time-Life International, New York.

Hall, E. T. (1959) *The Silent Language*, Doubleday, New York.

Hewes, G. W. (1973) 'The anthropology of posture', *Scientific American*, 196, 123-32.

Krout, M. H. (1954) 'An experiment attempt to determine the significance of unconscious manual symbolic movements', *Journal of General Psychology*, 51, 121–52.

Lodge, D. (1988) *Nice Work*, Secker & Warburg, London.

Lorenz, K. (1952) *King Solomon's Ring*, Methuen, London.

Lorenz, K. (1966) *On Aggression*, Methuen, London.

Mehrabian, A. (1972) *Nonverbal Communication*, Aldine Atherton, Chicago.

Morris, D. (1977) *Manwatching*, Jonathan Cape, London.

Morris, D. (1979) *Gestures*, Stein & Day, London.

Potter, S. (1970) *The Complete Upmanship*, Rupert Hart-Davis, London.

Scheflen, A. E. (1972) *Body Language and Social Order*, Prentice Hall, Englewood Cliffs, NJ.

Sommer, R. (1969) *Personal Space*, Prentice Hall, Englewood Cliffs, NJ.

Exercise 2

Try a series of experiments with your television set and video recorder:

1. Watch a news bulletin with the sound turned off and record it at the same time. Attempt to understand it as best you can and make notes of what you cannot follow. Then play the recording and check that you had understood properly, as well as filling in the gaps that the sound now provides.
2. A news bulletin is difficult, as convention dictates that the newsreader shall not use gesture or significant movement and shall be partly concealed by the news desk. Repeat the experiment with a section of a situation comedy or drama series. Then play the recording with the sound off and try to classify aspects of facial expression, gaze, gesture and posture that conveyed meaning, and the meaning that they conveyed. To what extent did you find that different actors used the same aspects of non-verbal communication to convey meaning?
3. Actors are relatively easy to 'read' as they are trained to express rather than conceal feelings. Repeat the full experiment with a section of a programme in which you can see people who are not trained performers, nor, like newsreaders, constrained by convention.

These experiments will develop your awareness of how people communicate, both deliberately and intuitively, by their body language. It will also enable you to begin a rough-and-ready classification to read the signals, although you will find that very few signals can be reliably read all the time. You may also notice composite patterns of behaviour, with several signals combining to convey a strong message. Frowning, flushing, snarling and banging on the table signal anger more reliably than any one signal in isolation!

Exercise 3

Try developing some behaviour composites that will convey your meaning to others. We have already had in this chapter a comment about different ways of reacting to someone who interrupts what you are doing. How do you get rid of people without being rude? Among the methods are the following:

- straightening the papers on the desk.
- sitting upright or some other marked change of position.
- putting both hands on the arms of the chair as if about to stand up.
- picking up a file, or some other signal of shifting attention to other business.
- looking at your watch.

Add to this list and then develop a repertoire of two or three combinations that may be used to close a conversation on your own territory, where you do not have the option of getting up and walking out, but neither do you want to cause offence.

Try them out and develop variations.

3 The basic skills: Listening and questioning

In handling face-to-face situations you speak, you listen and you question. This chapter is about the skills involved in all those activities, but especially the second and third. First there is a model of the communications process, then a section on listening skills and finally a series of questioning and associated methods for dealing with the range of situations that occur in face-to-face contacts.

Politicians who say in television interviews, 'I would like to make it perfectly clear . . . ' may be doing more to clarify their own thoughts to themselves than increasing the accuracy of the message received by the audience. They risk overemphasizing what they want to say rather than what is being heard and understood by the audience. In contrast, the manager who concentrates on feedback and listening will be clear to the audience, as the feedback and listening constantly monitor the accuracy of the picture being put together in the minds of the audience. A well-tried way of illustrating this is to use the analogy of telecommunications.

The communications model

Figure 3.1 shows that a person with an abstract idea to get across to someone else begins by encoding it. The idea is translated into speech patterns and actions to substitute for, or embellish, what is to be said. The signal is then transmitted by the words or actions being produced. The receiver picks up the message with some or all of his senses and decodes it. That decoding is not a simple mechanical process but an interpretation, and the code book used is that of the receiver's personal experience, expectation, trust, initial level of understanding and all the other factors that make for individual difference in perception. It is clearly in the encoding/decoding process that error will occur. The sender of the message will try to use a code that is appropriate to the receiver who will decode the message in its context. After decoding there is the final loop that closes the circuit of communication: feedback. The receiver gives some indication to the transmitter that the message has been received, and the nature of the response will usually indicate something of the quality of understanding.

Communication is therefore both mutual and circular, and feedback offers the opportunity for correction or reshaping of the original message. The sender can add to or alter the first message in order to clarify it and the receiver can test the decoding to make sure that the message registered is the message that the sender intended.

An example might be the thirsty man who approaches a bar. He encodes his thought by saying, 'A glass of beer, please.' His preoccupation with his own thirst is such that he provides little information apart from the bare necessity of beer. The bartender has little initial difficulty as people constantly come into the bar asking for beer. It is only the person asking for a glass of water who might be required to repeat the question. However, there are different sizes of glass and different types of beer, so there is a range of responses that will seek clarification of the original message:

- looking puzzled, to show that the message is insufficient.
- offering a choice – 'Half or a pint?'
- making a suggestion – 'A pint of best bitter?'
- seeking confirmation of a guess – 'A half of your usual?'

Each of these will lead to the feedback loop being completed by the bartender pouring what is required.

A further component of the communications process is 'noise'. That is anything that interferes with the quality of the message transmitted and received. We are all familiar with the experience of tuning a radio set to a signal in such a way as to avoid 'static'. In face-to-face communication the idea of noise can be used to cover all manner of things from the obvious problem of making yourself heard and understood above the sound of the pneumatic drill in the road outside, to the less obvious minor distractions of inattention, a familiar perfume that you cannot quite identify or wondering where he bought those shoes.

The competent manager gives careful attention to speaking, or transmission, making sure that the initial message is complete and couched in terms suitable to the receiver. This is not simply articulating clearly, it is also remembering who the receiver is and what the context is, including the problems of stereotyping, cognitive dissonance and the frame of reference considered in the first chapter.

Review topic 3.1

Tomorrow make a mental note of incidents during the day when someone else does not immediately understand what you say, or interprets you incorrectly. In the evening review each incident to work out what went wrong and how you could have avoided the problem.

Listening

To transmit effectively we have to listen carefully, because of the mutual and circular process that communication comprises. We have to be on the look-out for signals and willing to spend the time needed to listen and build understanding, deliberately holding back our own thoughts, which would divert or compete with the other's. This is unusual. If you eavesdrop on conversations, you usually hear two people competing with each other to speak rather than to listen. They are putting on a display, using the other person rather like a punch-bag. Careful and patient listeners are able to build on what the other is saying by planting their own ideas in the seed bed of what the other is interested in, or concerned about, and able to understand.

> Unfortunately, few people are good listeners. Even at the purely informational level researchers claim that 75 per cent of oral communication is ignored, misunderstood or quickly forgotten. Rarer still is the ability to listen for the deepest meanings in what people say. (Bolton, 1987, p. 30)

This ability to extract the real message from all the mass of material that is expressed has been called 'listening with the third ear' (Reik, 1948) and is almost the opposite of the man in the bar who provided too little information. Many people provide too much, largely by being bound up with their own preoccupations. The third ear enables the listener to pick out the significant elements and to discard the remainder.

We spend a great deal of time listening. Maude (1977, p. 106) cites studies showing that dieticians spend up to 63 per cent of the time listening and 22 per cent talking, while adult employees generally spend 42 per cent of their time listening and 32 per cent talking. Too often, however, our listening is passive, as we simply wait for the other person to finish.

Practical guidance on listening is provided by Sproston and Sutcliffe (1990). Here are some features of listening skill.

Tone of voice

Different feelings express themselves in different voice character-istics. An American counselling expert suggests the following probable meanings for various characteristics:

Characteristic	Probable meaning
Monotone voice	Boredom
Slow speed, low pitch	Depression
High voice, emphasis	Enthusiasm
Ascending tone	Astonishment
Abrupt speech	Defensiveness
Terse speed, loud tone	Anger
High pitch, drawn-out speech	Disbelief

Giving attention

We listen best by giving attention to what the other person is saying. As we saw in the last chapter, inclining the body towards the other person is a signal of attentiveness, so we need to remember our posture, which should be inclined forward and facing the other squarely with an open posture: folded arms can be inhibiting (Figure 3.1).

Figure 3.1 *An open posture indicates attentiveness. Folded arms can be inhibiting*

Eye contact is crucial to good listening, but is a subtle art:

> Effective eye contact expresses interest and a desire to listen. It involves focusing one's eyes softly on the speaker and occasionally shifting the gaze from his face to other parts of the body, to a gesturing hand, for example, and then back to the face and then to eye contact once again. Poor eye contact occurs when a listener repeatedly looks away from the speaker, stares at him constantly or blankly, or looks away as soon as the speaker looks at the listener. (Bolton, 1987, p. 36)

The distinction between 'focusing one's eyes softly' and staring is vital, though difficult to describe, and competence in eye contact is never easy to establish. It is one of the most intimate ways of relating to a person and many managers fear that the relationship may become too close. Even if you are happy with it, you may find that the other person is uncomfortable with you looking through the 'window' of their eyes.

We also show physical responses in our attentiveness. Firstly, we have to avoid distracting the other person by physical behaviour that is unrelated to what is being said: fiddling with a pen, playing with car keys, scrutinizing our fingernails, wringing our hands, brushing specks of dust off our sleeves are a few typical behaviours that indicate inattention. Skilled listeners not only suppress these, they also develop minor gestures and posture variants that are directly responsive to what the other is saying.

Silence

Being silent helps you to listen by providing space for incoming messages; but it also provides opportunities to observe the other person and to think about what is being said. Most people are uncomfortable with silence and try to fill it with inconsequential chat, but this interferes with listening. Being silent, and deliberately leaving verbal lulls in face-to-face situations, provides the opportunity for the other person to say more – perhaps more than was initially intended.

Silence still has to be attentive and the longer the silence, the harder it is to be attentive: think of the last lecture you attended and how hard it was to maintain attentiveness.

Silence may be necessary while someone processes a new thought. A question posed in performance appraisal, for instance, may be greeted with initial silence. The unwise interviewer will fret about having disconcerted the respondent and will fill the silence by suggesting the answer, or rewording the question, when in fact the respondent needs the silence to produce a considered answer. Mayerson (1979, p. 120) suggests that 30 seconds is not too long to leave a silence:

> it is more helpful at first to let the silence happen. There is a temptation to fill it up as if it were an empty basket. This has negative effects, especially if the silence is a productive one or one of great feeling . . . . The length of time one should let silence alone is arbitrary. It depends on the cues one is getting and one's own comfort with the situation. A very general rule of thumb is 30 seconds. That is a long time. More than 30 seconds lets everyone forget what was happening, and takes the participants away from the emphasis or the subject.

Review topic 3.2

Consider the following sayings:

- 'The audience were on the edge of their seats.'
- 'She gave me the cold shoulder.'
- 'He remained poker-faced throughout.'
- 'Speech is silver; silence golden'.
- 'She is down in the mouth today.'
- 'He was all ears.'
- 'She is a stuck-up person.'
- 'He is on his high horse.'
- 'Her face lit up.'

What do these suggest to you about effective and ineffective listening?

Reflection

In reflection, the listener picks up and re-states the content of what has just been said. Beveridge provides an excellent summary of its use in counselling situations:

> a selective form of listening in which the listener picks out the emotional overtones of a statement and 'reflects' these back to the respondent without any attempt to evaluate them. This means that the interviewer expresses neither approval nor disapproval, neither sympathy nor condemnation. (Beveridge, 1968, p. 72)

At a more prosaic level, reflection provides indication of listening: that you are attending to what the other person is saying, have understood it and are providing the opportunity for any misunderstanding to be pointed out. The standard method is paraphrasing, by which the listener states the essence of what has been said. This is done concisely and gives the speaker a chance to review what has been said.

Mayerson (1979) describes a similar tactic as empathic feedback. An example of how this would be done is in the following exchange:

RESPONDENT: Seniority does not count for as much as it should in this company.

REFLECTION: You feel there is not enough acknowledgement of loyalty and long service?

Alternative reactions would have a different effect, for example: 'You sound like someone who has been passed over for promotion', or 'Oh, I don't know about that.' Both push the respondent on to the defensive, expecting a justification of what has been said. Another alternative: 'Well, I think seniority has been overemphasized in the past' – stifles the opinion before it has been fully expressed. The respondent who is diffident will not develop the feeling further, so the matter cannot be resolved. There is also the danger that any one of these evaluative reactions could evoke a comeback from the respondent which complies with the view suggested by the interviewer. This is the same problem as that of the leading question, which is dealt with shortly.

Questioning and associated methods

We now move to consider specific aspects of method in communication by setting out a number of ploys, grouped into five categories – opening, questioning, feedback, closing and pitfalls – that can be used to handle different stages of the interactive situations described in later chapters.

Opening

Interactions usually open with a degree of skirmishing as each party assesses the other and tunes in. This is followed by more subtle behaviours to support the relationship and maintain the credibility of the attitudes that were demonstrated at the beginning.

Rapport: Enabling the participants to interact effectively
This is the sort of thing most people do quite instinctively a dozen times a day: 'Hello, how are you today?' 'Can't complain. How are

you?' 'Not so bad for the time of year, I suppose. Be better by five o'clock.' 'Ha, won't we all! Well, see you later.' 'Right, cheers.' That type of ritual conversation takes place on staircases and in changing rooms regularly, and the same pair of people will say the same things to each other day after day, but they have 'bonded' at the beginning of a new day and the fact that their exchange is always the same has a certain reassurance about it. In interviews and committees, however, there is greater formality in the exchanges which makes this stage of the proceedings more important than in casual encounters, especially when strangers are meeting for the first time, as in most employment interviews and much selling.

All parties will have an interest in setting up rapport, but in the more formal situations it is the duty of the clear controlling figure – the selection interviewer, the counsellor, the tutor – to take the initiative. Candidates do not expect to have to put selectors at their ease. Here are some of the standard methods.

(a) Small talk

The staple component is small talk that does not matter in substance. Most common is to discuss the weather, so that the participants can use an innocuous topic to exchange words and sounds while assessing the other's personality and beginning to relax in the presence of their counterpart.

(b) Friendly, easy manner

This is much easier to advocate than to produce. In many of the situations explored later in this book, the person not directing the interaction will be wary or ill at ease. Allaying that suspicion will nearly always help the conduct of the meeting, so that exchanges become more frank and informative. The first step is to show friendliness in the opening display, but that will have to register with the receiver as friendliness and not as condescension, falseness or casual indifference. This is difficult to do and most problems occur with people who try too hard and come across as insincere.

(c) Calm attention

The interviewer who is able to project a feeling of calm and quiet will win a response from the other person more quickly and construct-ively than the interviewer who deliberately or unwittingly conveys an atmosphere of busyness and preoccupation. The manager who can create an unhurried atmosphere will complete the encounter more quickly than the person who emphasizes that only a few minutes are available. Paying attention to what is being said will focus the thinking and responses of the other person.

(d) Explaining the procedure
In any interaction the respondent will be uncertain about what is to
happen, through being dependent on the other to direct proceedings.
The interviewer can build rapport by explaining aspects of the
process – how long the conversation is likely to take and what the
interviewer would like to accomplish are useful here. If the
respondent is to take an initiative at any stage, this is usefully
signalled now: 'There will obviously be questions that you want to
ask, and there will be plenty of time for that later on.'

We must ensure that establishing rapport is not mechanical, but a
ritual that is used to make the interaction work. An example of
falseness in rapport exchanges is the health-service administrator
who opened each selection interview with a question about the
candidate's journey. As each person replied with one of the normal
variations of 'Very nice, thank you', he reacted with a standard,
hearty 'Splendid!' Unfortunately he produced the same 'Splendid!'
when one candidate told him that she had had a puncture and arrived
ten minutes late. Another example is an earnest interviewer of
school-leavers applying for jobs in a well-known bank who always
exchanged pleasantries for three minutes with a strained smile before
changing expression to one of pained disapproval and saying, 'Well, I
think we've established rapport, so I will proceed with the questions.'

Reward: Sustaining the smooth interaction with the respondent
Rapport does not take too long or it becomes laboured. After a very
few minutes the conversation moves to the substance that the two
people have come together to discuss. It is important, however, that
the interviewer does not leave behind the warm and responsive
behaviour displayed at the beginning: that has to be maintained
throughout the encounter. Some of the conventional methods are
given here.

(a) Interest
We all respond positively when a listener is interested in what we are
saying, so the manager will encourage and draw out the respondent
by showing interest in what is being said. If it is possible also to agree
with what is being said, the reinforcement of the respondent will be
greater.

(b) Affirmation
A talker is always looking for the affirmation of the listener in order to
complete the feedback loop in the communication circuit. The most
common form is the head nod, and many public speakers look for

head nods as a way of judging the supportive mood of the audience. Other ways of affirming are the use of the eyes. This is too subtle and individual to describe, but we each have a repertoire of signals to indicate such reactions as encouragement, surprise and understanding. When the eyes are part of a smile, there will be stronger reward to the talker. There are also words and phrases: 'Really?', 'Go on . . . ', 'Yes . . . ', 'Of course . . . ', 'My word . . . ', 'You were saying . . . '.

(c) Noises

Conversation contains a variety of noises that are ways of rewarding the other party. They are impossible to reproduce in words but are usually variations on a theme of 'Mmm . . .' and they form a part of the conversation that is inarticulate yet meaningful, and keep things going without being interruptions.

Exploding: Bringing latent, suppressed feelings into the open

This last, melodramatically named ploy is for use in those specialized situations where there is some pent-up feeling that the interviewer believes should be expressed early in order to clear the way for subsequent discussion. It is used in discipline or grievance settlement on occasions, but is less common in other encounters.

(a) Letting off steam

Many managers ignore signals of frustration in respondents because they do not want to get into a difficult or contentious situation, and the warning signals are disregarded. If, however, a respondent is showing obvious signs of anger or distress at the start of an encounter, it can be helpful to encourage the blow-up and the rush of feeling that follows. It will not solve the problem, but it will at least make the rest of the conversation more constructive.

(b) Digging

Sometimes the anxiety or disappointment in the respondent is latent but not expressed. There may still be a need to try and bring out the disquiet to the surface in order to prevent it worsening. The signals are harder to read and will probably only be seen by someone who knows the respondent well, who may then try a sally like, 'There seems to be something on your mind?'

Questioning ploys

Questioning obviously takes up a large part of most face-to-face situations; but questions are of different types, so the competent manager is able to classify questions into different types and work out the appropriate way to use each type.

Closed Questions: Questions seeking precise, terse information
When we want precise, factual information we close the question to control the answer:

- 'Is it Clarke with an *e*, or without?'
- 'Who is in charge?'

These are useful when you want clear, straightforward data, and most encounters feature closed questioning at some point.

Open-ended Questions: Questions avoiding terse replies, and inviting respondents to develop their opinions
Here the respondent is invited to speak without having the interviewer prescribe what the answer should be. The question does little more than introduce a topic to talk about:

- 'How are you getting on?'
- 'What does your present job entail?'
- 'What are your future plans?'

Open-ended questions often come at the beginning of an encounter as a means of developing the rapport. It makes things easy for the respondent, who is given latitude to decide what to talk about, with the opportunity to relax and get going. Their main purpose, however, is to obtain the type of deeper information that the closed question misses, as the shape of the answer is not predetermined by the questioner. You are informed not simply by the content of the answers, but by what is selected and emphasized.

Direct Questions: Questions 'insisting' on a reply
Now the manager is asserting his or her authority and the 'right to know'. Direct questions use the prescriptive style of the closed question but seek fuller information of the type that open-ended questions usually deliver, unless the respondent is being evasive:

- 'Did you take the money?'
- 'Why did you leave that job?'
- 'Did you, or did you not, clock Charlie Miller in yesterday?'

Indirect Questions: Questions taking an oblique approach on a difficult matter
These have the same general objective as direct questions but take an indirect approach. Higham illustrates how an indirect question can be a more effective approach than the direct alternative:

What were your colleagues like in that job?' is preferable to 'Did you get on all right with the rest of the office?' But the virtues of the indirect question go further still. A blunt 'Did you like that job?' almost suggests you didn't, or at least raises the suspicion that the interviewer thinks you didn't! Put indirectly as 'What gave you the most satisfaction in that job?', it has the merit of concentrating on the work rather than the person. (Higham, 1979, p.134)

Probes: Questioning to obtain information that the respondent is trying to conceal

This is not so much a style of questioning as a tactical sequence to deal with those situations in which supportive and encouraging interviewers can be deflected by respondents who are not to be cajoled, by the winning ways of reward and open-ended questions, into divulging information they prefer to conceal. When this happens the questioner has to make an important, and perhaps difficult decision: do you respect the respondent's unwillingness and let the matter rest, or do you persist with the enquiry. Reluctance is quite common in disciplinary and grievance interviews, where someone may be reluctant to criticize a colleague, and in employment interviews there may be an aspect of the recent employment history that the candidate wishes to gloss over. The most common sequence for the probe takes the following form.

(a) Direct questions

Open-ended questions give too much latitude to the respondent, so direct questioning is needed. Careful phrasing may avoid a defensive reply.

(b) Supplementaries

If the first direct question produces only evasion, then a supplementary will be needed, reiterating the first with different phrasing.

(c) Closing

If the probe is used when the rapport is well established, it stands the best chance of being successful, but it then needs to be closed skilfully. If the information has been wrenched out like a bad tooth and the interviewer looks horrified or sits in stunned silence, then the respondent will feel put down beyond redemption (Figure 3.2). The interviewer needs to make the divulged secret less awful than the respondent had feared, so that the encounter can proceed with reasonable confidence. For example: 'Yes, well you must be glad to have that behind you.'

Figure 3.2 *Looking horrified is likely to make the respondent feel put down beyond redemption*

There is a dirty trick that can be used as an alternative method of probing. Although no reader of this book would ever dream of using this tactic, it is described below so that you can see it coming if anyone tries it on you.

(d) Overstatement
If a suggestion is put that implies a reason for the reluctance that is more grave than the real reason, then the respondent will rush to correct the false impression.

Q: There appears to be a gap in the employment history at the beginning of last year. You weren't in prison or anything, were you?
A: Good heavens, no. I was having treatment for . . . er . . . well, for alcoholism, actually.

A thoroughly dirty trick, but effective.

Proposing Question: A question used to put forward an idea
This is for feeling a way out of an impasse, and is to be found in negotiation, brainstorming and other situations where there is difficulty in pulling people together. It is a ploy to test for consensus

without being so positive that it then has to be defended if consensus does not emerge:'Well, now that we have the consultant's report shall we accept Helen's earlier suggestion'? This is a tactic either for the acknowledged leader in a group, or it is a bid for leadership by one member challenging the rest to disagree.

Rhetorical Question: A question 'forbidding' a reply

This is really a way of making a statement, as it poses a question in such a way that the answer is too obvious to state. Replying to a mixture of allegations about incompetent behaviour, a manager might ask: 'How can we be slack on purchasing procedures and too strict on reorder levels, both at the same time?'

Feedback

There is one ploy to be mentioned under this general heading, although some of the main behaviours have already been described under reflection, rapport and reward.

Summary and rerun: Drawing together in summary various points from the respondent and obtaining confirmation

The respondent will produce lots of information in an interview and you will be selecting that which is to be retained and understood. From time to time you interject a summary sentence or two with an interrogative inflection:

- 'You did take the wallet out of his locker, then, but this was because he had asked you to fetch it for him so that he could repay Charlie his fiver?'

- 'So the difficulty in meeting the sales target has been more to do with production problems than with customer demand?'

This tactic serves several useful purposes: it shows the interviewer is listening, gives the respondent the chance to correct any false impressions; and reinforces the key points that are being retained. It is also a useful way of making progress, as the interjection is easily followed by another open-ended question – 'Now perhaps we can turn to . . . '

Review topic 3.3

Recall a recent face-to-face situation in which you were involved – an interview, a discussion, a *tête-à-tête*, a lesson, an argument. Identify three ways in which the other person was especially effective, and analyse why. Then think of three things about your own performance that did not seem to be effective. What were these?

Braking and closing ploys

Most of the suggestions so far have been to encourage a response, but it is easy to nod and smile your way into a situation of such cosy relaxation that the respondent talks on and on and on, rather like lying back in a warm bath. Also, there are a surprising number of interviewers who can begin an interview smoothly but have great difficulty closing, so there are two ploys to suggest.

Braking: Slowing the rate of talking by the respondent

You may eventually need to become peevish with the overtalkative respondent, but braking provides a sequence of less drastic techniques to shut people up. You will seldom need to go beyond the first two or three, but five are offered in case you have to deal with a really tough case, like a university lecturer or someone selling you double glazing.

(a) Closed questions
It has already been pointed out that closed questions invite terse replies. One or two interjected to clarify specific points may stem the tide.

(b) Facial expression
The brow is furrowed to indicate mild disagreement, lack of understanding or professional anxiety. The reassuring nods stop and the generally encouraging, supportive behaviours of reward are withdrawn.

(c) Abstraction
If the respondent does not notice the change of facial expression, the next step is for the eyes to glaze over, showing that they belong to a person whose attention has now shifted away from the respondent and towards lunch or last night's football match.

(d) Looking away

To look at one's watch during a conversation is a very strong signal indeed, as it clearly indicates that time is running out. Most people are very reluctant to do it and often an interviewer will take the watch off beforehand so as to be able to look at it discreetly during the interview. An alternative is to keep it on your wrist so that you can look at it more obviously and so slow down a verbose respondent. Other milder ways of looking away are: looking for matches or glasses, looking at your notes or looking at the aircraft making a noise outside the window (Figure 3.3). A rather brutal variant is to allow your attention to be caught by something the respondent is wearing – a lapel badge, a tie, a ring or piece of jewellery, maybe. Putting on your glasses to see it more clearly is really rather unsporting!

Figure 3.3 *Looking away can slow the rate of talking by the respondent*

(e) Interruption

The most blunt of methods. Most people avoid it at all costs, but in the end you have no choice.

Closing: Finishing the interview without 'closing' the respondent

In closing an interview future action is either clarified or confirmed. Also, respondents take a collection of attitudes away with them, and these can be influenced by the way the encounter is closed, particularly after counselling or disciplinary interviews. There is a simple procedure:

(a) First signal, verbal plus papers
The interviewer uses a phrase to indicate that the interview is nearing its end:

- 'Well now, I think we have covered the ground, don't you?'
- 'I don't think there is anything more I want to ask you. Is there anything further you want from me?'

In this way you signal the impending close at the same time as obtaining the respondent's confirmation. There is additional emphasis provided by some paper play (Figure 3.4). A small collection of notes can be gathered together and stacked neatly, or a notebook can be closed.

Figure 3.4 *Paper play can signal the impending close*

(b) Second signal, explaining the next step
The interviewer confirms what will happen next:

- 'Can we meet again next week, to see how things are proceeding?'
- 'There are still one or two people to see, but we will write to you no later than the end of the week.'

(c) Closing signal, stand up
As the ground has been prepared, all that is now required is the decisive act to make the close. By standing up, the interviewer forces the respondent to stand as well and there remains only the odds and ends of handshakes and parting smiles.

Pitfalls

Some common behaviours can produce an effect that is different from what is intended.

Leading Questions: Questions that suggest what the 'correct' answer should be
These will not necessarily produce an answer which is informative; what they will produce is an answer in line with the lead that has been given:

- 'Would you agree with me that . . . '
- 'I believe in strict control of expenditure and firm handling of debtors: what about you?'

Unless you are really using the question rhetorically, leaders are of little value, and can be misleading in the replies they produce.

Unreasonable Exhortation: Expecting a change in emotional state as a result of complying with an instruction
This is a commonplace which does more for the person doing the exhorting than for the person who is exhorted because the change that is sought is rarely a simple matter of will (Figure 3.5):

- 'Stop crying.'
- 'Relax.'
- 'Cheer up'.

Multiple Questions: Questions that give the respondent too many inputs at one time
These are sometimes found when interviewers are trying very hard to efface themselves and let the respondent get on with the talking, so

Figure 3.5 *An instruction does not always result in a change of emotional state*

there is an occasional attempt to put a number of questions together. The idea is to provide the respondent with a stock to draw on when ready: 'Well can you just tell me why Fred threw the spanner at you, if it really was Fred; what you did when you saw it on the floor; and what on earth the start of all this silly horseplay was?' However helpful the interviewer intends to be, the effect is that the respondent will usually forget the later parts of the question, feel disconcerted and ask, 'What was the last part of the question?' By this time the interviewer has also forgotten, so they are both embarrassed.

Taboo Questions: Questions that infringe the reasonable personal privacy of the respondent
Although there is a proper place for the probe, there are some questions that have to be avoided, usually in selection interviews, as they could be interpreted as discriminatory. It is at least potentially discriminatory in selection, for instance, to ask women how many children they have and what their husbands do for a living. Questions about religion or place of birth are also to be avoided, as they imply that certain types of religious affiliation or ethnic origin are desirable or undesirable.

Also, some questions may do no more than satisfy the idle curiosity of the questioner. If there is no point in asking them, they should not be put.

Mechanical Behaviour: Routine questions that never vary, with contrived, stilted reactions to the respondents' replies

Mechanical behaviour is suitable for some situations, where carefully phrased closed questions, developed over years of experience, efficiently produce precise information. This is appropriate, for instance, for those registering births and deaths, or for the initial stages of many medical investigations. Most managerial encounters need to go further than this because there is a working relationship to be created, sustained or repaired.

References

Beveridge, W. E. (1968) *Problem-Solving Interviews*, Allen & Unwin, London.

Bolton, R. (1987) *People Skills*, Simon & Schuster, Brookvale, New South Wales.

Higham, M. (1979) *The ABC of Interviewing*, Institute of Personnel Management, London.

Maude, B. (1977) *Communication at Work*, Business Books, London.

Mayerson, E. W. (1979) *Shoptalk: Foundations of managerial communication*, Saunders, Philadelphia.

Reik, T. (1948) *Listening with the Third Ear*, Grove Press, New York.

Sproston, C. and G. Sutcliffe (1990) *Twenty Training Workshops for Listening Skills*, Gower, Farnborough.

Exercise 4

You need a partner for this exercise, so that you can take it in turns to lead and respond. You can also involve a third person as observer, if you find this helpful. You are going to practise some of the skills described in the chapter.

1. Listening/summary and rerun
You both spend one or two minutes separately preparing a brief statement on a controversial issue.

- You make your statement to your partner.
- Your partner restates what you have said, reflecting and summarizing it as accurately as possible.
- You make any necessary corrections until you are satisfied that your partner understands your point of view and has summarized it accurately.

Now repeat the exercise, but swap roles.

2. Asking open-ended questions/follow-up questions
Now you are going to ask questions that will keep your partner talking purposefully and informatively for five minutes. You both prepare one or two open-ended questions on how something is done in your partner's organization.

- You put an open-ended question to your partner and develop the reply with follow-up questions.
- You put your second question and develop the reply in the same way.

Now repeat the exercise, but swap roles.

After five to ten minutes ask the observer to comment on the amount of focus and development that was offered, how it was used and the general effectiveness of the exchange.

3. Asking closed questions
Now try to find out as much as you can in one minute about your partner's job, hobby, last summer's holiday or some other topic on which you are ignorant, but your partner is well informed. Agree on each topic and then work out a series of questions to produce the information you need.

- Take care with the phrasing of questions to produce clear answers.
- Take fifteen minutes preparing your list.
- Put your questions, limiting yourself to sixty seconds in total.

Repeat the exercise, having swapped roles.

Ask the observer to initiate discussion between the three of you on the relative effectiveness of each enquiry by comparing the amount of information disclosed.

Note of Caution
This is an exercise to identify different types of technique and to practise them. It is not suggested that you should conduct 'real' encounters with carefully prepared questions.

4 Structure and types of face-to-face situation

The purpose of the interaction determines how it should be handled. If a manager faces a discussion with a group of shop stewards about a conflict of interests, it is the conflict which needs to be addressed. It is damaging to ignore that very difficult task by talking blandly about 'all being in the same boat' and needing 'to pull together'. That ignores the realities of the situation in which the manager is in a position of holding considerable organizational power in relation to the stewards. When dealing with peers, managers have a different aspect of organizational power to consider: how to influence people whose motivations are different.

> A lack of understanding regarding the communication rules of a particular relationship or situation may be the most serious of all possible breakdowns. Rules are the basis on which the communication relationship must be constructed. If mutual understanding regarding the expectations of each participant can not be achieved, then it becomes impossible for interpersonal communication to occur. (Baskin and Aronoff, 1980, p. 35)

Russell (1972, cited in Baskin and Aronoff, 1980) examined the degree of understanding between one hundred sales representatives and their immediate superiors in their communications together. His findings show the problems: in 60 per cent of situations there was what Russell called monolithic consensus as both parties to the interaction agreed on the communications rules and their perceptions. In 20 per cent of situations there was a false consensus, which meant that the participants disagreed, but believed they agreed. Pluralistic ignorance was the position where the parties agreed without knowing it and dissensus was where the parties disagreed and knew it. Both of these last two categories accounted for 10 per cent of the responses.

Types of interaction

The remainder of this book is organized by putting a number of common interactive situations into four distinct categories: finding out, putting it over, joint problem-solving, conflict resolution (Figure 4.1). From the point of view of managers developing their skills, it

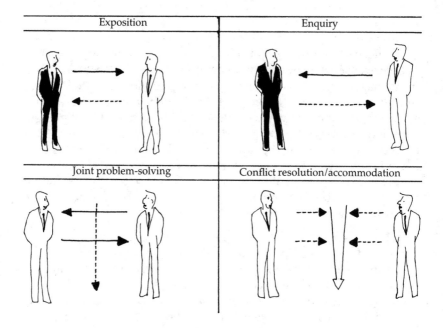

Figure 4.1 *Four categories of interaction: exposition, enquiry, joint problem-solving, conflict resolution/ accommodation*

seems to be helpful to follow the logic of these categories in approaching the different situations, as this can clarify thinking about what is to take place and give a sharper focus to the ensuing discussion. The categories are, however, frameworks for action rather than watertight compartments. Selection interviews, for instance, are mainly for finding out about candidates, and the selection interviewer who does not clearly direct the interview to find out about candidates will disorientate the candidates as well as making some strange selection decisions. The same interviewers, in the same interviews, will also spend time providing information and perhaps trying to persuade candidates of the value of working in the organization.

Finding out

Here the manager has the main job of finding something out, obtaining rather than imparting information. The manager does not know 'the answer' beforehand, but has to discover it. In the telecommunications analogy, the manager is the receiver rather than the transmitter; but finding out obviously involves more than simply tuning in to a signal that is being transmitted: the transmission has to be stimulated in the first place.

In working life the standard example is the selection interview. The manager needs to know a lot of things about the candidate, so that task is to obtain that information. Other examples are investigating a problem, where a number of people have to be questioned in order to gather the necessary data to understand the difficulty and its probable causes, finding out about a new product or a new customer. There will be a great deal of feedback, and the candidate will have as many unanswered questions as the manager, but the main job of the manager is finding out.

Further examples are attitude surveys, market-research interviews, the analysis of training needs, preparing job descriptions and carrying out health checks. The effectiveness of the interaction will depend on the accuracy with which the manager can build the picture in his or her own mind of what is in the mind of the other person.

The chief skill in finding out is questioning, to ensure that information flows mainly from the respondent to the manager. Some information will still flow from manager to respondent, so as to provide an acceptable base for the questions to be put and then to provide focus for the answers that are being offered. In this way the respondent is led to provide the requisite information. The market-research interviewer, for instance, will have to provide some information at the beginning of the encounter to persuade the respondent to stop and consider the questions. Once the respondent has agreed to participate, the researcher can move on to the questions, but the questions themselves will be worded to contain a steady flow of information as to what is needed. This produces replies that are accurate and informative.

Putting it over

The opposite of finding out is where the manager's main task is to convey information or ideas to one or more other people. The manager knows 'the answer' so the task is to transfer that as accurately as possible into the minds of the listeners. This is the simplest example of the communications process, with all the stress on encoding, sending the signal and collecting the feedback to test accuracy and modify later signals. The emphasis is completely on the manager to make things clear and put the message over.

There are many examples. There is the one-word instruction 'Fire!' and the many similar perfunctory orders: 'Take this down to Mr Jones', 'Get another one from Stores', 'Offer them another 2.5 per cent if they settle this week.' As communications, these are not too difficult, but in the same category are more complex skills, like reporting back, briefing, public speaking and lecturing. In these situations the manager has to work harder at the exposition, with greater clarification and perhaps the need to convince the respondents against their better judgement. Greater skill is required on these occasions, but the task remains that of putting it over, transferring a message outwards.

Joint problem-solving

The third category is quite different, as 'the answer' is not known to either party before the interaction begins. The task of the manager is not, therefore, to concentrate on accurate transfer of a picture from one mind to another, but rather to use an exchange of information to create a picture, which is helpful to both parties but beyond the power of either to create single-handedly. It is a collaborative activity, requiring not only both participants to work together, but also a degree of mutual trust as each supports the other in a shared quest for understanding, which is a preliminary to making decisions and taking action. It is both more complex and more complete than interactions in the first two categories.

A useful example is career-development interviewing, where the management development officer or personnel manager has a responsibility to ensure that the respondent employee is making the expected contribution to organizational objectives. The respondent is perhaps a management trainee, wanting to know what progress is being made towards the glittering prizes at the top of the hierarchy, or whether career direction should be altered in some way. They have to come together to talk about what is happening as each knows only a part of the story at the outset. They need to exchange information from their two different points of view, as 'the truth' of the matter lies in the composite picture, of which separately they can only provide some components. Often the manager will have to begin by clarifying mutual expectations, as the respondent will be looking for a clear, straightforward answer to the question 'How am I doing?' without the need for preliminary discussion.

Other situations turn out unexpectedly to be joint problem-solving. The question over the telephone, 'Can I call in and get you to explain this new pension scheme for a few minutes?' may turn out to be, 'I can't make up my mind about whether or not to take early retirement.'

Conflict resolution

The final category is the most complex and time-consuming inter-action of all, resolving – or finding an accommodation for – conflict. As with joint problem-solving it is an interaction where 'the answer' is not known beforehand and the participants have to come together to fashion it. The fundamental difference is the low level of common interest, as the parties are seeking objectives which, to some extent, are against the interests of each other. The buyer of an aero-engine will seek the lowest possible price, while the seller will seek the highest possible price: they cannot both be completely satisfied. Neither, however, will seek their own ends at all costs. The buyer will want the seller to remain profitably in business, continuing with research and development, and the seller will not want to obtain one order but lose later opportunities because of overcharging. Although the opening positions of the two parties are seen as the optimum for each, they both have to take account of the opposing position in order to find a balance between their conflicting aims after testing the logic and strength of the opposition through open argument.

There is not the same clear leading role in conflict resolution as in other encounters, as the parties see themselves as being evenly matched; although in some cases the lead is taken by a third person holding the ring. Arbitration and mediation are examples of this.

Sometimes these encounters are between individuals with third-party involvement, as described by Walton (1969). Usually, however, they are collective activities with teams representing each side, as in negotiations between managers and shop stewards. Typically, great emphasis is placed on following procedures and observing ritual requirements.

For the next part of this book a series of different interactions in each of these four categories is examined in detail.

Three stages of interaction

The main, loose framework for these ten chapters is the three stages of preparation, encounter and follow-up, with a sequence for each of the three stages. The sequence is at least logical but will sometimes need to change, as the performances we are discussing are those which depend for their success on individual ability, flair and judgement. They also depend on the people involved, the organizational culture and the economic context in which you are operating. The suggested sequencing should not therefore be regarded as a tightly belted straitjacket allowing no variation. On the other hand, it should not be altered without thinking through the implications of such variation.

References

Baskin, O. W. and C.E. Aronoff, (1980) *Interpersonal Communication in Organizations*, Goodyear., Santa Monica, CA.

Walton, R. E. (1969) *Interpersonal Peacemaking: Confrontations and third party consultation*, Addison-Wesley, Reading, MA.

5 Finding out: The selection interview

Selection interviewing is rather like ballroom dancing in its heyday, when close physical co-ordination was necessary and one person was absolutely dependent on the other. The applicant in selection depends on the control and direction of the interviewer, but most interviewers are as incompetent as the legions of tone deaf and flat-footed young men who trod on the toes of their helpless partners during the quickstep, despite the strict tempo of the dance band.

Ballroom dancing has now become a pastime only for the expert, who is willing to train to reach an acceptable standard. This is not possible in selection interviewing, which can seldom be restricted to trained enthusiasts. If the production manager is recruiting an assistant, both have to meet and make a mutual assessment, no matter how incompetent the production manager may be at inter-viewing. Also there is no clear criterion of success in interviewing against which trainee interviewers can be measured. An apparent criterion is 'getting the right person in the right job', but how can you judge when a person is right, and how do you know that others who would have performed better have not been turned away?

Books and training sessions for applicants, teaching them how to present themselves, only have limited value because control lies with the interviewer and our social conventions require the applicant to follow that lead, however ineffective the leader.

Ritual in selection

Selection is an interaction where ritual elements are most marked, as the applicant is seeking either to enter, or to rise within, a social system. This requires the display of deferential behaviours: 'upward mobility involves the presentation of proper performances and . . . efforts to move upward . . . are expressed in terms of sacrifices made for the maintenance of front' (Goffman, 1972, p. 45). At the same time those who are already inside and above display their superiority and security, which are made the sweeter by the appearance of someone so obviously anxious to share the same privileged position. Reason tells us that this is inappropriate and inhumane, as it produces an unreasonable degree of dependency in the applicant; and the books (including this one) are full of advice to interviewers not to brandish their social superiority, but to put applicants at their ease and to reduce the status differentials. Even this, however, acknowledges their superiority, as they are the ones who take the initiative; applicants are not expected to help the interviewer relax and feel less apprehensive. Also the reality of the situation is usually that of applicant anxious to get in and selector choosing among several. Status differentials cannot simply be set aside. The selection interview is at least partly an initiation rite, not as elaborate as entry to commissioned rank in the armed forces, nor as whimsical as finding one's way into the Brownie ring, but still a process of going through hoops and being found worthy in a process where other people make all the rules.

Review topic 5.1

For a selection interview in which you recently participated, either as selector or as applicant, consider the following:

1. What were the ritual features?
2. Were any useful ritual features missing?
3. Could ritual have been, in any way, helpfully reduced?

Interview effectiveness

How reliable is the interview as a way of appointing the right people? For seventy-five years a series of research experiments have demonstrated its weaknesses, but its use remains almost universal:'The reliability is generally found to be dubious and the validity very disappointing and suspect . . . . Nevertheless it remains the most widely practised method of selection' (Lewis, 1985, p. 150). The main criticism is summed up by Webster (1964). After extensive research he showed four main weaknesses:

1. Selectors tended to decide for or against a candidate within no more than three or four minutes of the interview beginning. They then spent the rest of the interview looking for evidence to prove their first impression accurate.

2. Selectors formed tentative opinions on the basis of the application form and the appearance of the applicant; these were seldom altered by the interview itself.

3. When the selector has made up his mind, in the first few minutes, his subsequent behaviour betrays that decision to the candidate.

4. Selectors place more weight on unfavourable than favourable evidence.

The value of Webster's comments is to provide pointers of what to avoid. The selector tempted to be unduly influenced by the initial impression that an applicant gives or gives off, can reduce that by self-discipline. The easiest change is to shift the balance of evidence that is solicited away from the unfavourable towards the favourable.

Review topic 5.2

For the next selection interview you conduct, write yourself some notes (now) on the following:

1. how you will avoid making a snap yes/no judgement in the first few minutes.
2. how you will concentrate on using the interview to collect evidence about the applicant, deferring any judgement until later.
3. how you will ensure that you collect evidence to show why you should appoint the applicant as well as evidence for rejection.

The value of the interview

It is worth reviewing some benefits of the interview, despite the criticisms:

1. The interview can be a key part in the process of deciding between different candidates for the same vacancy.

2. Applicants expect an opportunity to put their own case to a person or panel, rather than be judged entirely by objective methods.

3. The interview is an efficient way of clearing up points of factual uncertainty on both sides, such as clarifying exactly what the applicant was doing for two years in Peru or explaining the mysteries of the management-development programme.

4. The interview is a logical conclusion of the employment process as information from a variety of sources – the application form or

c.v., references, test results, the personnel specification and job description – can be discussed together and some assessment made of those intangible issues, like whether or not two people could work harmoniously together, that cannot be approached by any other way.

The interview is crucial in the employment process and when it is criticized for its unreliability, the criticisms do not constitute an argument for abandoning it: they constitute an argument for improving it. Apart from Webster, some of the most helpful research on interviewing is by Mayfield (1964), Lopez (1965) and Arvey and Campion (1982).

Approaches to the selection interview

Selection interviews are sometimes conducted by panels of several people and in other situations it is a one-to-one discussion. The individual interview gives the best prospect for meaningful interchange, rapport, trust and efficient use of time, as there are only two trains of thought to be dealt with. Applicants usually find this process the easiest to cope with, as they do not have to adjust constantly to different questioners. The drawback is the considerable dependence on the judgement of one selector, though this may be eased by the use of a series of single interviews.

The panel interview is intended to ensure justice is done by requiring decisions to be made collectively by a group of people following discussion among them. It has the advantage that the decision is made quickly and there is no doubt that the ritual requirements are fully met, but does it produce sound decisions? The drawback is the inevitable inflexibility of the encounter and the status differential of a panel sitting in judgement on the humble submission of the applicant. There is little prospect of building rapport and developing a discussion; instead, applicants are fed a series of prepared questions, to which they offer answers that may also have been prepared. In several local education authorities, for instance, the candidates are told beforehand the questions that they will be asked, so that the interview becomes an audition as panel members sit silently appraising the performance. Because the panel members are so constrained, and perhaps apprehensive about the preferences their colleagues may have, the apparent 'fairness' of the process is often undermined by attempts to get the decision effectively made before the interview, which is 'only a formality'. This suborning is done by informal, one-to-one interviews beforehand, the exchange of confidential telephone calls to swap opinions and mild lobbying of panel members to ensure the appointment of X.

Most selection interviews have one of three dominant modes. First is the stress interview, where the inevitable applicant anxiety is deliberately heightened by the selector in order to apply pressure. This is justified by an idea that it will reveal weaknesses, demonstrating an orientation in the selector to look for the unfavourable, as Webster pointed out. Evaluating people's behaviour under stress is problematical and it is doubtful if it can be done adequately by other than skilled interviewers.

Secondly, opinion-soliciting is where the selector has a string of questions on which the applicant's opinion is sought – 'Who should have responsibility for passing invoices, purchasing or accounts?' or 'How can you get a good balance between controlling what people do and giving them free rein?' The difficulty here is the same as with stress – how do you evaluate the evidence? How important are the opinions expressed by applicants in interview? They are predisposed to be sycophantic and can do no better than present hasty, ill-informed opinions. For posts where a particular set of values are seen as appropriate, detailed discussion of applicants' views would be necessary. It could be useful to clarify applicants' views on smoking if they were to be involved in advertising cigarettes, or opinions on aspects of government policy if the interview was for the headship of a school.

The third mode, the biographical interview approach, is the safest and usually the most productive, as the discussion ranges over what the applicant has actually done. The objectives of this are clear, the progression logical and what lies behind the question is less open to interpretation, so that gamesmanship is reduced. The information already provided on the application form is enlarged and enriched as the selector builds up a full picture of what the applicant has done, and this is more accurate than trading spontaneous value judgements or contriving artificial stress. The following sequence assumes the biographical approach.

The selection interview sequence

Preparation

(a) Selector briefing
The selector will study first the job description, which will have set down the details of the job to be done by the person appointed.

Where there is no such document, it will be necessary to review the general understanding of what is required. Then there is the personnel specification, in which the ideal appointee is described. Together these provide a picture of the job to be done and the sort of person envisaged for appointment. Then come the application forms or *curricula vitae* for scrutiny. Assuming that there has been preliminary short-listing, the interviewer will check the match between what has been sketched in as the requirement within the organization and what is offered by the applicants. This matching helps the interviewer to work out some ideas on the main points for clarification and discussion in the interview itself.

(b) Timetable

The importance of timetabling is to make sure that applicants are fairly and effectively dealt with. A rigid timetable can end interviews arbitrarily at a predetermined time, frustrating those involved, or require another interview to be spun out for a further ten minutes, even though it has clearly finished already. At the other extreme, a highly flexible timetable can produce enervating periods of waiting by candidates. Nearly everyone reading this book will have had the experience of expecting an interview to start at, say, eleven o'clock and to be still waiting at 11.15 or 12.00. A junior hospital doctor seeking a post as registrar once commented that every minute you waited after the preordained time reduced your ultimate life expectancy by a year. Some people regard this as an occupational hazard that applicants must put up with, like waiting for the dentist, who does not keep you waiting on purpose but will sometimes be delayed because the previous patient is sick over the floor or grabs the drill and runs amok. Selectors are sometimes delayed in the same way. The flaw in this reasoning is that the dentist's patient has to do little after the delay but sit in a chair and be operated on. On the other hand, applicants in selection interviews have to perform: you want them in good, lively condition, not glassy eyed with fingernails bitten down to the elbow.

The best timetable is one which allows a break after each interview, with the applicants each arriving at different times. In most cases the selector has a few minutes to look through the papers and update notes, and the occasional interview can run late without any adverse effects. This arrangement also overcomes another horror, much beloved by some administrators, of asking all the applicants to arrive at the same time, so that Wilkinson sits for hour after hour as Adams, Evans, Jones, Phillips, Robinson and Smith are all dealt with.

(c) Reception and waiting

However much the selection process makes applicants feel their worthlessness, they are still making up their minds. Their acceptance of an offer of employment cannot be taken for granted and they will be looking for clues as soon as they enter the premises, forming opinions on whether or not it is a good place to work at.

Selectors will want to make all these initial impressions as favourable as possible, so it is worth briefing two people. First is the person on the door, who vets all visitors. Without briefing, this person may innocently confide to applicants that everyone in the building is mad and that he or she personally cannot wait for the passage of the next thirty-two days, after which they are retiring, never to set foot in the place again, not at any price. That same person, briefed by the selector, can become a cheerful participant in the recruitment process by adopting a quite different attitude.

The second intermediary is typically a secretary, who collects applicants and takes them to the interview location. The hazards here are those who do not speak once they have identified the visitor, but press on with silent preoccupation through long corridors trailing the hapless applicant behind, and those who speak to everyone else but the visitor, clearly believing that the applicant is not really there at all (Figure 5.1). Briefing can produce not only a different attitude, but also some useful information – 'When we get there I'll let you have a form for your expenses. Just post it back to me when you're ready.

Figure 5.1 *Trailing the hapless visitor behind*

They seem to be getting on quite well today. They've seen three people and there's one more after you.' The selector might, of course, collect the applicant personally so that the great uncertainty – what is the selector like? – is quickly done with.

Some time will be spent waiting for interview, although it will ideally be only a few minutes. In this time applicants will want to compose themselves and attend to what are known as personal needs. If they have to wait for more than ten minutes they would almost certainly welcome the offer of a cup of coffee.

(d) Setting

It is difficult but necessary to combine two features of the setting for the interview: what is right for the ritual and what is needed to enable a full and frank exchange of information. Amiable chats over pints in pubs are not fitting for the seriousness of the selection inquiry, though dinners in exclusive restaurants are a different matter, for some odd reason. If it is a one-to-one interview, the following are the main aspects of the setting to consider:

1. The room should be suitable for a private conversation, free of interruptions.

2. It should be clear where the candidate is to sit, with the selector and candidate on the same level and able to see each other easily.

There are also a range of obvious details that are often forgotten. Personal impedimenta of the candidate like sopping raincoats, umbrellas and bulging briefcases should be got out of the way; candidates should not face into bright sunlight and should not be ignored while the selector does something else. The following have been noted in recent years:

- A candidate being interviewed while still clad in full motor cycling oilskins and gloves. Eventually steam rising from the top made the selector suggest he might be more comfortable if he took them off.

- Candidates being seated in front of a glass door at the end of a corridor on the way to the staff canteen, so they were like dummies in a shop window.

- A candidate fumbling blindly for a collapsible umbrella that had fallen from her lap to the floor, while she never let her eyes move from the selector's face.

- A selector, standing with clip board in hand, who invited candidates to sit in any one of four chairs and then made a careful note of the one they chose.

- A selection panel for a local authority appointment who sat on the front row of the stalls in a repertory theatre, while the candidate sat in a deck chair, on the stage (Figure 5.2).

Figure 5.2 *The candidate sat on a deckchair on the stage*

- A selection panel in a different local authority where the chairman put the first question to the first candidate, whose answer was interrupted by the secretary saying: 'You will rise to address the panel, please.'

Encounter

Rapport
The opening of the encounter is when interviewer and interviewee make their preliminary mutual assessment. Details on method in rapport have already been provided in Chapter 3, but there are some points specific to the selection context.

A useful feature of the opening is to describe the procedure for the interview and its place in the total decision-making process. At the same time there is the opportunity for both to speak, to adjust their mutual intelligibility and to feel comfortable with each other. The outline of the procedure gives the applicant a framework to settle into, hearing what sort of interview to expect, how long it will take, whether there are other interviews to follow, how the decision will be made and when.

(b) Interview plan

Assuming that the interview is not to follow the format of stress or opinion-swapping, the natural basis for the exchange is the application form or c.v. The information on it has been supplied by the candidate and is in some logical sequence, if the form is set out correctly. An important general point about forms is to check the purpose for which they are intended. Are they a basis for the employment record or are they a basis for the interview? Some forms still exist that are clearly drawn up with personnel records in mind. There are boxes in which applicants have to write their national insurance number, their local tax office, whether they have been vaccinated and the name of their next of kin. If, however, the form is designed as a basis for the interview or the selection process generally, then applicants will be asked to provide information which is relevant to the yes/no decision that dominates that process, so it will be in a logical form and usually in biographical sequence. It is probably not helpful to start automatically with the applicant's childhood and work steadily through each stage until the present, but some logical sequence for the conversation is helpful, even if this is going backwards, providing that the logic is clear and predictable to the candidate as well as to the selector.

The opening question is crucial to the success of the interview. The best point at which to start is the applicant's present job ('Could you give me a general outline of your present responsibilities?'), as it is both a question for which applicants will be prepared, and one on which they will be knowledgeable. Some suspicious selectors regard this as too vague and easy (what is wrong with easy questions?) and like to sharpen it up by saying something like, 'I'd like to get a general idea of a typical day. What did you do yesterday, for instance?' The applicant will regard that as very limiting and will try to break out of the restriction. In doing this there is the beginning of 'improving' on the truth by switching in something that sounds good but happened last week, and switching out the half hour spent yesterday afternoon surreptitiously watching the football on the television in the rental shop next door. The slippery slope of deception has begun already: the selector has turned the encounter into a battle of wits.

Another poor, but very common, opening is, 'Why are you interested in this job?' That is threatening because the reasons for the application are often complex and not easy to summarize. Also they include reasons which applicants do not feel it wise to declare, like more money, more power, longer holidays, an easier life and an opportunity to escape from the hopeless mess that they are making of the job they are in. The result is again deception ('Well, quite frankly, I'm looking for a bigger challenge. I feel I have more to offer than is required of me in my present post'). It will have an element of truth in it, but will be exactly what the selector has heard everyone else say. The opening must get the conversation started on the basis of honest statements about real stuff.

Important elements of the plan will be key issues and check points. Key issues will be the main two or three features of the application form that stand out as needing elaboration or clarification. A particular episode of previous employment may need to be explored to see the range of responsibilities held, the number of subordinates, the difficulty of the circumstances. There may be key issues relating to education, experience in other countries or in specific industries that were noted by the interviewer in preparing for the interview. Check points are matters of detail needing clarification: dates of an appointment, grades in an examination, rates of pay being some of the more common ones.

(c) Observation

Although the encounter is a conversation, information will not only come through what is said. The selector will collect some data by watching. Notes can be made about appearance, dress, height and weight, if these are likely to be important, and there will be at least some clues of change in the applicant's emotional state from non-verbal behaviours.

(d) Listening

Although the interview is for the applicant to pick up information as well as the selector, applicants expect most of the information to flow from them, as it is their opportunity to 'sell themselves'. To do this they need to talk, so selectors have to curb their own talking and concentrate on listening.

(e) Questioning

The various types and categories of questions are described in Chapter 3, but the art of questioning depends upon the personality and style of the selector, who will develop an individual technique through a sensitive awareness of what is taking place. Anstey describes this as the apotheosis of interviewing skill: 'Once rapport has been established, the actual questions matter less and less. The candidate senses what one is getting at, without worrying about the form, becomes increasingly at ease and responds more spontaneously'(Anstey, 1975, p.103).

(f) Notes

If notes are made on the application form they can be written around the information the applicant has already provided and are then easier to understand afterwards (Figure 5.3). Some selectors feel inhibited about taking notes in case it impairs the smoothness of the interaction, but all that seems necessary to prevent any difficulty is to develop a knack of jotting down points throughout the conversation without interrupting. The more one listens instead of talking, the easier note-taking becomes.

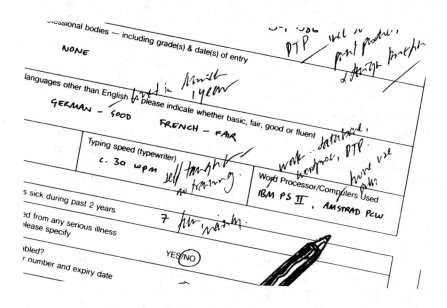

Figure 5.3 *Making notes on the application form can add to the information already provided by the candidate*

(g) Control

Remember the flat-footed ballroom dancer at the beginning of this chapter. The applicant will expect the changes to be controlled by the selector, who has to keep things moving, ensuring a brisk, business-like pace: winding up discussion in one area and moving to another, heading off irrelevant reminiscences and bringing in the probes for matters that have been glossed over.

Follow-up

(a) Decision

After all the interviews, the selector or panel members decide to whom an offer will be made. They have not decided during the interviews themselves, if they remember Webster's criticism. Also they do not decide about individual applicants between interviews as that pre-empts the later interviews. The decision is made by the simple process of matching what is wanted (job description and personnel specification) against what is offered (information about individual candidates) and deciding on where the best match lies. There have been a number of attempts to put decision-making on a more systematic basis and many readers will be familiar with the classic works of Rodger (1952) and Fraser (1978) that have advanced schemes which have been widely adopted. It is not easy, however, to find evidence of these schemes being used in a disciplined way by contemporary interviewers. One recent piece of research (Keenan, 1976) investigated the work of company representatives visiting British universities to interview third-year undergraduates with a view to offering employment. The most important characteristic reported in the decision-making of these interviewers was 'pleasant personality'.

A summary of the Fraser method is given in Table 5.1.

(b) Corroboration

When the decision is made there will be some corroboration of the facts that have been mentioned by the applicant. Customarily, applicants do not wish their current employers to know of their attempts to find other employment, so they ask for the proceedings to be kept confidential. In that case the corroboration can only take place after the offer has been made.

It is difficult to see any justification for collecting opinions from referees after the decision has been taken and the offer made. If this is to be done at all, the opinions should be collected before the interview or at least before the decision is finalized. It is, however, perfectly reasonable to check on the main facts of what you have been told. Furthermore, if candidates know that facts will be corroborated, they will probably stick very close to the truth in what they say.

(c) Notifying the unsuccessful

It is important to let the unsuccessful know. A sizeable minority of employers do not bother and this not only seems unreasonable to the applicants, it also gets the employers a bad reputation in the labour market.

Table 5.1 *Making selection decisions*

J.M. Fraser devised a five-fold framework for selection decisions that enables selectors to organize their general understanding of the people they have seen.

Use the form below to organize your thinking about candidates, marking A, B, C, D or E in each box, with A meaning much above average, E meaning much below average and B, C, D providing the intermediate steps.

	Candidates				
	1	2	3	4	5
Impact on others, or the kind of response a person's appearance, speech and manner calls out from others.					
Qualifications and experience, or the skill and knowledge required for different jobs.					
Innate abilities, or how quickly and accurately a person's mind works.					
Motivation, or the kind of work that appeals to a person and the amount of effort they are prepared to put into it.					
Emotional adjustment, or the amount of stress involved in living and working with other people.					

Table 5.2 *The selection interview sequence*

Preparation

1. Review:
   - job description;
   - personnel specification;
   - application forms or *curricula vitae*.
2. Check:
   - timetable
   - setting.

Encounter

1. Begin with:
   - rapport.
2. Plan:
   - logical sequence;
   - careful opening question;
   - key issues and check points.
3. Find out by:
   - observation;
   - listening;
   - questioning;
   - making notes;
   - keeping control.

Follow-up

1. Decide.
2. Corroborate.
3. Notify the successful and unsuccessful.

References

Anstey, E. (1975) *Techniques of Interviewing*, Barry Rose, London.

Arvey, R.D. and J. E. Campion (1982) 'The employment interview: A summary and review of present research', *Personnel Psychology*, 35, 281–322.

Fraser, J. M. (1978) *Employment Interviewing*, 5th edn, Macdonald & Evans, London.

Goffman, E. (1972) *The Presentation of Self in Everyday Life*, Penguin, London.

Keenan, A. (1976) 'Interviewers' evaluation of applicants' characteristics', *Journal of Occupational Psychology*, 49, 223–30.

Lewis, C. (1985) *Employee Selection*, Hutchinson, London.

Lopez, F. M. (1965) *Personnel Interwiewing*, McGraw-Hill, New York.

Mayfield, E. C. (1964) 'The selection interview: A re-evaluation of published research', *Personnel Psychology*, 17, 239–60.

Rodger, A. (1952) *The Seven Point Plan*, National Institute for Industrial Psychology, London.

Webster, E. C. (1964) *Decision-making in the Employment Interview*, Industrial Relations Center, McGill University, Montreal.

Exercise 5

For this exercise you need a co-operative, interested relative, or a very close friend, who would welcome interview practice.

1. Follow the sequence suggested to give your partner practice in being interviewed for a job, and giving yourself practice in interviewing and note-taking.

2. Discuss your mutual feelings about the process around questions such as:

   Selector
   - Did you ever feel you were being misled? When? Why?
   - Did you feel the interview got out of your control? When? Why?
   - How could you have avoided the problem?
   - How was your note-taking?
   - What, if anything, made you bored or cross?
   - What did you find most difficult?
   - How comprehensive is the data you have collected?

   Candidate
   - Were you put at your ease?
   - Were you at any time inhibited by the selector?
   - Did you ever mislead the selector? When? How?
   - Did the selector ever fail to follow up important points? When? Which?

- Were you in any way disconcerted by the note-taking?
- Has the selector got a comprehensive set of data about you, so that you could feel any decision made about you would be soundly based?
- What did you think of the interview experience?

3. Now swap roles.

6 Finding out: The attitude survey

The common view of the attitude survey is the poll of electoral opinion or the questioning of shoppers about their brand preferences in supermarkets. There are, however, many more applications in organizational life of this type of tightly structured interview. Examples are in job analysis and job evaluation, work study, training-needs analysis and market research, as well as the assessment of employee opinion about prospective changes in working practice or payment arrangements.

There is a clear difference between the method of finding out in an attitude survey and the method of the selection interview that we considered in the last chapter. The emphasis in selection is on the single situation and the lone candidate from whom the selector is collecting enough data to put together a full, rounded picture. In the survey interview the investigator is sampling a population and seeking data that is useful only in aggregate. The survey is to identify a relatively small number of pieces of precise information with emphasis on ensuring consistency of responses. This requires considerable preparation and discussion of exactly what questions will be asked and how they will be worded, including trial runs to test questions. Also, the respondent is pushed into an inflexible pattern of response, with none of the relaxed free-wheeling of the selection interview, in which they selector is always trying to fit the interview around what the candidate is wanting to say. Closed questions are the norm; open-ended questions are rare.

This technique of finding out is thus quite different from that of selection, even though it is concerned with the same basic task of collecting information. The survey can predict quite accurately how a large number of people will respond in a given situation: which one of several possibles they will select as their Member of Parliament, how they would respond to a change in the method of payment, or how many would join a trade union if it were recognized by the management. It can also reveal dimensions of present behaviour that are not otherwise known: what people find most difficult in their jobs, whether they understand the payment scheme, whether they have confidence in their management. It is this area of employee attitude that has seen the biggest growth of surveys in recent years:

> Most surveys tend to be specific, focusing on a particular issue; surveys linked to customer care programmes, seeking both to reveal attitudes and to stimulate suggestions, and quality audits are examples; even more specifically assessments can be carried out of house newspapers or of video presentations on annual results, or information can be gathered in order to design or install new machinery. (Hogg, 1989, p. 85)

Whatever the particular application, the common aim is standardization of the information obtained:

> the schedule standarized interview in which the wording and order of all questions is exactly the same for every respondent, the purpose being to develop an instrument that can be given in the same way to all respondents. All the questions must be comparable, so that when variations between respondents appear they can be attributed to actual differences in response, not to the instrument. (Denzin, 1970, p. 123)

Review topic 6.1

For which of the following would an attitude survey be an appropriate method of finding out:

1. the sales prospects of a new line in cutlery;
2. the most popular dates for a company close-down at Christmas;
3. suggestions for improving company management;
4. the value of team briefing in a company;
5. methods of combatting football hooliganism?

One of the preconditions for accurate responses is that the respondent should feel confident in the neutrality of the inquirer, so that answers will be truthful and informative, rather than answers that sound right but may be misleading:

> Managements who have carried out such surveys themselves have frequently, and understandably, encountered bias in the answers they received from their employees, since the latter do not feel completely free to express their views. The survey is of little value

unless such inhibitions are removed. Respondents must feel able to talk freely and frankly, secure in the knowledge that the results of the survey will be presented in such a way that complete anonymity is guaranteed. (North and Buckingham, 1969, p. 51)

Survey interviews involve more premeditation than others covered in this book, as the interviewer is usually one of several, all trying to achieve consistency between each other in reporting.

The attitude survey sequence

Preparation

(a) Objectives
In deciding what the inquiry is to discover, we begin by considering what this form of inquiry *can* discover. Denzin (1970, pp. 123–4) lists four underlying assumptions:

1. Respondents have a sufficiently common vocabulary so that it is possible to formulate questions which have the same meaning for each of them.

2. It is possible to find a uniform wording for all questions that is equally meaningful to every respondent.

3. For the meaning of each queston to be identical for each respondent, the sequence of questions must be identical.

4. Careful pilot investigation, development and pretesting will provide a final schedule of questions that meets the requirements of the first three assumptions.

For the inquiry to be successful the respondents must, therefore, be a population with sufficient in common to meet the requirements of the first two of these assumptions. Also, the information sought must be of the type that can be reduced to precise units of response to standard questions.

(b) The interview structure
The most detailed, practical advice for survey interviewers is in a booklet produced by the British Office of Population Censuses and Surveys, and the following check list for drafting an interview structure is based on suggestions in that publication (Atkinson, 1978, p. 16):

1. What will be the respondents' reaction to the subject of the survey? Responses to questions about payment arrangements are

likely to be more guarded than responses on the (slightly) less sensitive topic of catering facilities.

2. How can the subject be presented to respondents to achieve a high response? In-company investigations are less likely to have problems with response rate than those conducted among the public at large, as the respondents are almost a captive population, but even a small proportion of refusals can reduce the reliability of the results.

3. What is the best order in which to introduce topics? In a survey there is the need to begin with questions that are easy for respondents to understand and reply to accurately, as well as getting them 'on the wavelength' of the inquiry before proceeding to more complex questions.

4. What wording of questions will produce precise data? Here are the considerations of vocabulary and semantics with the need to use words that are not only unequivocal, but also where the meaning is not likely to drift with the respondent. Another consideration is the distinction between questions to obtain facts and questions to seek opinion. There is more on this topic in the section of this chapter dealing with the Encounter.

5. How long can the interview last? The need to know has to be balanced with the ability of the respondent to reply. Some respondents will not be available to answer questions for long periods, others will have difficulty in maintaining concentration and others will have much more to say than the interview schedule provides for. Also, survey interviewers may suffer from fatigue and lapses in concentration when repeatedly asking identical questions.

6. What is the best layout of the survey forms? Answers to the five questions above enable those organizing the inquiry to prepare forms that are convenient for the inquirers to use in the variety of situations in which they are asking their questions.

Review topic 6.2

When you are approached by a market-research or similar interviewer, what is likely to make you agree to be interviewed and what is likely to make you refuse? How could the interviewer deal with your refusal?

(c) The pilot study

A pilot study tests the suitability of the provisional interview structure. The interview is conducted with a small sample of respondents to test the various points on the above check list. Some words will be found insufficiently precise to stimulate the particular type of response that is needed. Certain topics will be more difficult and others easier than was anticipated at the planning stage. Timings will be monitored and – most important – the data collected will be analysed to establish that it is producing what is required. The number of interviews required for a successful pilot cannot be decreed out of the context in which the main study is to take place, but it will probably be necessary to pilot between 5 and 20 per cent of the ultimate number of interviews required, depending upon the complexity of the survey and the eventual number of interviews to be conducted.

(d) Preliminary analysis

The results produced by the pilot are analysed in order both to modify the structure and to prepare the final analysis methods. The first is achieved by checking that the questions are producing the kinds of answer required and that there is no inconsistency between the results recorded by different interviewers. The information received will also suggest additional questions because of potential in the inquiry that the designers of the structure had not realized earlier. This does not mean that the survey will be structured according to what the respondents want to say, but that ways of discovering information may turn out to be through different questioning approaches as well as through different wording of questions.

Preliminary analysis will require consultation with those who have sponsored the inquiry — key managers, a committee, a group of shop stewards or whoever it is who brought the inquiry into existence in the first place and who might call it off if developments are different from those anticipated.

Preliminary analysis prepares for final analysis by bringing in changes in the layout of interview forms to ease the collection of data from the forms and coding some of the responses whereby respondents are offered a range of alternatives from which they select one that is identified by a code number or letter.

Encounter

The dominant feature of survey encounters is their fleeting and anonymous nature. Two strangers meet as one asks questions of the other, with both knowing that they will soon part and forget each other. The transient and impersonal nature of the encounter leads to a degree of frankness in answers that would be less likely if respondents did not appreciate the quasi-mechanical nature of the interviewer's participation and the fact that their own replies had no meaning other than as part of an aggregated, depersonalized accumulation of data:

> As an encounter between . . . two people the typical interview has no meaning; it is conceived in a framework of other, comparable meetings between other couples, each recorded in such fashion that elements of communication in common can be easily isolated from more idiosyncratic qualities. However vaguely this is conceived by the actual participants, it is the needs of the statistician rather than of the people involved directly that determine much, not only the content of communication but its form as well. (Benney and Hughes, 1956, p. 141)

(a) Self-presentation
The interviewers have a strange part to play in this encounter, as they need to present themselves positively enough to engage the attention of the respondent, who may initially be reluctant, at the same time as effacing themselves to ensure the appropriate anonymity that the encounter demands. Those engaged to conduct surveys of public opinion are usually required to dress in a carefully calculated manner to emphasize their blandness and to de-emphasize their individuality. Denzin (1970, p. 140) offers a simple dictum: 'dress in a mode of dress most acceptable to those being interviewed but employ a style that communicates who you are with respect to them.'

(b) Introduction
Before the interview can begin, the interviewer has to provide certain information to get the respondent 'in play'.

1. The purpose of the survey. What it is intended to achieve and by what means. This will usually include comment on the authorization of the investigation (e.g. 'the Works Council felt it would be helpful').

2. How the respondent came to be selected for interview. Sometimes in-company surveys cover all members of the prospective population who are willing to be interviewed, but usually representatives are identified and respondents need to know why they have been picked out.

3. The confidentiality of the investigation. The anonymity of the data has to be explained, especially if the interview is to begin with factual information that to some extent identifies the respondent. This is only to categorize the data, but it may seem to the respondents that they are immediately being personally identified.

4. The fact that the respondent is a volunteer. Respondents always have the opportunity to decline, even though the interviewer may try to persuade them to co-operate. The unwilling respondent is of little value (Figure 6.1) and usually gives distorted information as a result of this reluctance. If it is made clear that they are being invited to take part rather than being required to, then their co-operation is more likely and their answers will be more helpful.

"I JUST WANTED TO ASK A FEW QUESTIONS..."

Figure 6.1 *The unwilling respondent is of little value*

5. How long the interview will take. This information should be accurate, so that respondents get into the appropriate mode of response. If they think it will take five minutes, their degree of concentration will be less than if they think it will take half an hour.

(c) Dealing with non-cooperation

If it is true, as has been suggested above, that unwilling respondents are of no value, this might imply that the interviewer accepts a refusal without comment and tries another respondent. Interviewers cannot, however, too readily take 'No' for an answer, as the resulting information may not be truly representative of the population. Alternatively, the refusal may be based on misapprehension. Some people may be sufficiently timid or of such short service with the organization that they feel their contribution would be of little value.

When there is initial reluctance it may be overcome by further clarification of the reasons for the investigation. If a reason for the refusal is offered, the interviewer has a basis for a further attempt. Some typical refusals and counters are as follows:

Refusal	Counter
1. 'Well, I'm afraid I am rather busy at the moment.'	'That's all right. I'll call again when it is more convenient. Would sometime tomorrow morning be all right?'
2. 'I don't hold with all this survey business; it's a waste of time and money. My opinions are my business and no-one else's.'	'Well, it is absolutely confidential, and I know that (they) are going to use these results quite fully.'
3. 'I've only been here a week, mate. Nothing I could tell you.'	'We do need to get responses from people with all sorts of length of service. People who have been here for a few days notice things that others don't.'
4. 'Oh, I don't know. Try someone else.'	'We need to get as clear a picture as possible of what everyone thinks and your views would be especially helpful.'

Some of these will work most of the time, but not always. Other refusals are more confounding because they throw doubt on the care with which the operation has been planned:

- 'He's left'.
- 'He's dead'.
- 'It's Miss, actually, not Mrs.'
- 'There's nobody called Warrington, but my name's Farrington.'
- 'It's the first I've heard about it. They tell you nothing in this place. "Consultation?" – they couldn't even spell it.'

(d) Putting the questions
Suggestions here are again based on the comments of Atkinson (1978, p. 94).

1. Know the interview form. The investigator needs to know the layout of the form before starting and needs to be able to scan forward from the question being asked to those that are coming up. This produces a smooth sequence of question and answer without the personality of the investigator obtruding, and ensures that the appropriate time is being allowed for each question.

2. Put questions precisely as instructed. They must always come in the predetermined order and using the standard wording so that variation in questioning is not a cause of varying data.

3. Use linking patter. Questions are probably grouped and the interviewer needs to prepare respondents for the move from one group to another; otherwise the new question may be misheard due to the respondent still being on a different wavelength.

4. Avoid assumptions about replies. Interviewers have to cope with the tedium of eliciting many similar responses, but there is a risk of assuming what the reply is without having actually heard it. If twenty people have produced an identical response the twenty-first may sound identical but in fact only be similar.

5. Use prompts to ensure consistency. Prompting is a way of suggesting an answer and is sometimes built into the question itself, by offering an example of the sort of thing the question is looking for. On other occasions the interviewer uses prompts to jog a person's memory. The important thing is that prompting should be done consistently and by prior agreement among interviewers.

6. Watch for misunderstandings. Sometimes respondents are so bound up with the answer they have just given that they misinterpret the next question and hear it wrongly, producing an incongruent answer. The usual way to deal with this is to repeat the question with as little overtone as possible. If the question is put again in another way there is the inevitable risk of distorting the response.

(e) Control and recording
The interviewer has to control the encounter without having much flexibility, as the interview cannot stop before the form is satisfactorily completed. There will be some voluble respondents who provide

more information than is needed. In these situations the interviewer has to mention time limitations or make some flattering remark about the respondent's views being varied and interesting, providing a breadth of perspective that is very welcome, but at the moment there are some specific (not more interesting) questions to be answered. Where respondents produce answers that are incomprehensible, the interviewer makes it clear that it is the interviewer's naïveté and lack of experience that make the answer meaningless. The respondent will then delight in making things clear to the novice.

An American study by Cannell *et al.* (1978, pp. 205–24) suggests the following features that affect the reliability of responses:

1. Time lapse: as the time between an event and the interview increases, there is increased under-reporting of information about that event.

2. Salience: events important to the individual are reported more accurately than those of less importance.

3. Social desirability: reporting of an event is likely to be distorted in a socially desirable direction.

4. Event-specific recall: the accuracy of responses is improved by relating questions to specific events.

The same study produces evidence to support the view that reliability can be improved by reinforcing behaviours from the investigator (e.g. 'Thanks, this is the kind of information we want'), and by getting the respondent to make an overt agreement to work hard at providing complete and accurate information.

Data from the respondent is recorded when it is provided; not recalled later. Many responses call for no more than a tick in a box or a circle round a number, so that the interviewer feels like a talking machine, but it is important to place the ticks and circles accurately. Where something is to be written in, it is written exactly as it is spoken: it is not paraphrased or condensed, although there may be a range of standardized abbreviations, like DK for 'don't know'.

Review topic 6.3

What issues in your own company could be usefully investigated by an attitude survey, without risking the problem of uncovering information that it would not be possible to deal with? Have attitude surveys been used recently? Was there any apparent result?

Table 6.1 *The attitude survey/sequence*

Preparation
1. Ensure:
   - common vocabulary of respondents;
   - uniform wording for all questions;
   - identical sequence of questions;
   - pilot study.
2. Structure the interview by considering:
   - respondents' likely reaction to the subject;
   - presentation for high response;
   - the order of topics;
   - the wording of questions;
   - the length of the interview;
   - layout of the form.
3. Complete:
   - pilot study;
   - preliminary analysis.

Encounter
1. Present yourself to the respondent.
2. Introduce the survey by providing the following information:
   - purpose of the survey;
   - how the respondent was selected;
   - confidentiality;
   - the respondent as volunteer;
   - time required.
3. Deal with potential non-cooperation.
4. In putting the questions:
   - know the interview form;
   - put questions precisely as instructed;
   - use linking patter;
   - avoid assumptions about replies;
   - use prompts to ensure consistency;
   - watch for misunderstandings.
5. Control and record.

Follow-up
1. Analyse the data.
2. Write the report.

Follow-up

(a) Data analysis

When all the interviews are complete and the forms gathered together, they are counted and sorted. Then the analysis of the data begins. The first stage is counting numbers and this is most likely a computerized operation as the straight data is picked up from the forms and fed into the machine for analysis and permutation.

(b) Report-writing

Having processed all the numbers, a report has to be written to show what the facts mean and how they are related. The information has to be understood and then explained in the report by means of a theory which makes sense of the data. The final, and crucial, stage of the report is producing some conclusions about future action which the interpretation of the facts illuminates.

References

Atkinson, J. (1978) *A Handbook for Interviewers*, 3rd impression, HMSO, London.

Benney, M. and E. C. Hughes (1956) 'Sociology and the interview', *American Journal of Sociology*, 11 (September), 137–42.

Cannell, C. F., L. Oksenberg and J. M. Converse (1978) 'Striving for response accuracy: Experiments in new interviewing techniques', in R. Ferber (ed.), *Readings in Survey Research*, American Marketing Association, Chicago.

Denzin, N. K. (1970) *The Research Act in Sociology*, Butterworths, London.

Hogg, C. (1989) 'Attitude surveys: Factsheet 21', *Personnel Management*, 21 (9), (September), 85.

North, D. T. B. and G. L. Buckingham (1969) *Productivity Agreements and Wages Systems*, Gower, London.

Exercise 6

1. Identify a small group of people who you think will collaborate with you, either from where you work, where you live or in some other grouping, like a squash club or a darts team.
2. Pick a topic on which they will all have some knowledge, such as quality of a bus service they all use, canteen meals, what constitutes a good darts player, etc.
3. Decide three or four aspects of their attitudes on which you want to collect information.

4. Prepare your questions for a short interview (5–10 minutes) and your form to record their answers.
5. Approach them without forewarning, win their agreement to take part, put the questions and examine the outcome.
6. Analyse the results and then feed back your findings to the group together, discussing with them their reaction to your approach.

7 Putting it over: Training or skill

Training methods have developed rapidly in recent years and there is greater emphasis on development as opposed to inculcation. Management training is centred on working in groups, action learning, discovery and concentration on the learner rather than the teacher. This chapter deals with an approach to training that has received little emphasis of late, but which remains the method most widely used for training in manual and clerical skills. It would not be appropriate for more advanced skills or for developing knowledge.

Teaching a person to do something is different from teaching someone to understand something. In this chapter we are going to consider how you train someone to do something. This broad distinction between training in skill and training in knowledge has been refined by the Comprehension, Reflex, Attitude, Memory, Procedural (CRAMP) taxonomy (ITRU, 1976), developed after a study of the work of the Belbins (Belbin and Belbin, 1972). This system divides all learning into five basic types.

- *Comprehension* is where the learning involves theoretical subject matter, knowing how, why and when certain things happen. Examples would be the laws of thermodynamics or the currency structure of the European Monetary System.

- *Reflex* learning is involved when skilled movements or perceptual capacities have to be acquired, involving practice as well as knowing what to do. Speed is usually important and the trainee needs constant repetition to develop the appropriate synchronization and co-ordination. Obvious examples are juggling and gymnastics, but the use of a keyboard is the most obvious of the many examples to be found in organizations.

- *Attitude development* is enabling people to develop the capacity to alter their attitudes and social skills. Much of the customer care training currently being conducted has this as its basis.

- *Memory* training is obviously concerned with trainees remembering how to handle a variety of given situations. Pharmacists learn by rote a series of maximum dosages, for example, and an office messenger will need to remember that all invoices go to Mr Brown and all cheques to Mrs Smith.

- *Procedural* learning is similar to memory except that the drill to be followed does not have to be memorized, but located and understood. An example is the procedure to be followed in shutting down a plant at Christmas, or dealing with a safety drill.

Most forms of training involve more than one type of learning, so that the apprentice vehicle mechanic will need to understand how the car works as well as practising the skill of tuning an engine, and the driver needs to practise the skill of co-ordinating hands, feet and eyes in driving as well as knowing the procedure to follow if the car breaks down. Broadly speaking, however, comprehension-type learning is best approached by a method that teaches the whole subject as an entity rather than splitting it up into pieces and taking one at a time. Here the lecture or training manual are typically used. Attitude change is now often handled by group discussion to which there is reference in the final chapter of this book, but reflex learning is best handled by part methods, which break the task down into sections, each of which can be studied and practised separately before putting together a complete performance, just as a tennis player will practise the serve, the smash, the forehand, the backhand and other individual strokes before playing a match in which all are used. Memory and procedural learning may take place either by whole or by part methods, although memorization is usually best done by parts.

Review topic 7.1

Think back to a time when you learned a lot in a short time, such as a change of job, new responsibilities or coping with a new piece of equipment, like a computer terminal.

1. What most helped you to learn?
2. Was it comprehension, reflex, attitude, memorization or procedural learning?
3. How was effective performance reinforced?

Reflex learning of motor skills

The first step in learning a skill is for the trainee to understand the task and what needs to be done to produce a satisfactory perform-ance. This provides the initial framework for, and explanation of, the actions that are to be developed later, although more information will be added to the framework as the training proceeds. The job of the tutor at this point is to decide how much understanding is needed to set up the training routine, especially if part methods are to be used for the later practice.

An elementary skill is the pouring of molten lead into moulds to produce a 'grid' that forms the basis of a lead–acid battery plate. To avoid waste and personal hazard a trainee will practise pouring sand instead of lead for a short spell. The trainee who does not understand the reason for pouring sand while training for a job in which lead is to be poured will not bring much application to the practice. The tutor will therefore need to explain that feature. Trainees are usually keen to get started with 'hands-on' experience, so long and detailed preliminaries are best avoided.

The second step is to practise the performance, so the tutor has to decide how to divide the task up into separate units or subroutines to aid learning. Typists begin their training by learning subroutines for each hand before combining them into routines for both hands together, but pianists spend very short periods of practice with one hand only. The reason for this seems to be that typists use their two hands in ways that are relatively independent of each other with the left always typing 'a' and the right always typing 'p', so that co-ordination of the hands is needed only to sequence the actions. In playing the piano there is a more complex integration of the actions performed by the two hands, so separate practice can impair rather than enhance later performance. A further aspect of learning to type is to practise short letter sequences that occur frequently, such as 'and', 'or', 'the', 'ing' and 'ion'. These can then be incorporated into the steadily increasing speed of the typist. A feature of this type of development is the extent to which the actions become automatic and reliable. The amateur typist will often transpose letters or hit the wrong key, writing 'trasnpose' instead of 'transpose' or 'hte' instead of 'the'. The skilled typist will rarely do this because the effect of the repeated drills during training will have made the subroutines not only automatic but also correct.

The third element is feedback, so that trainees can compare their own performance with the required standard and see the progress they are making. The characteristics of good feedback are immediacy and accuracy. If the feedback comes immediately after the action the trainee has the best chance of associating error with the part of the performance that caused it, whereas delayed feedback will demonstrate what was wrong, but the memory of what happened will have faded. The boy learning to bowl straight at cricket will immediately be able to see how accurate his attempt was, and will be able to connect the degree of deviation with the position of his feet, the angle of his arm or whatever caused the problem. The trainee photographer does not have that element of immediate feedback.

The second characteristic of feedback is that it should be as accurate as possible in the information it provides on the result and the performance. The person coaching the trainee cricketer may say, 'That's pretty good', or may say, 'That was the best ball so far, but it was still an inch or so too wide. Try to keep your arm higher as you bring it over.' The second comment provides a general indication of making progress, it provides an assessment of the performance and specific comment that should improve the next attempt. Fitts and Posner (1967) elucidate this very helpfully.

The training for skill sequence

Preparation

(b) Objectives

The trainer will have two sets of objectives, organizational and behavioural. Organizational objectives specify the contribution to the organization that will be made by the trainee at the end of training. It will be general but necessary. If a company trains its own typists, for instance, it might be that the organizational objectives will be to teach people to type and to transcribe from handwritten copy or dictating machine, but not to take short-hand. These are different from educational objectives, which focus on the trainee or student rather than on organizational needs, so that tutors in secretarial colleges are more likely to organize training around what will be useful in a number of occupational openings. The tutor will need to work out organizational objectives which may or may not include broader educational features.

Behavioural objectives are specifically what the trainee should be able to do when the training, or training phase, is complete. Organizational objectives for typist trainees may be simply to ensure a constant supply of people able to type accurately and at reasonable speed. In behavioural terms that would be made more specific by setting standards for numbers of words to be typed to a predetermined level of accuracy per minute.

Review topic 7.2

Think of a training experience involving learning how to do something that you are contemplating for yourself or for someone else in your organization. Note down organizational objectives and behavioural objectives for the training.

(b) Learning methods

Next the tutor will decide what learning methods are to be used. We have already seen that the main elements of skill training are understanding, practice and feedback; so the tutor decides how much initial explanation is needed, and how many other explanations at different stages of the training, together with the form that is appropriate. Words alone may be enough, but audio-visual illustration and demonstration will probably be needed as well. There are rapid developments in computer-based training and interactive video that can provide frequent explanations and feedback on trainee performance (Rushby, 1987)

The two questions about practice are to decide on the subroutines and any necessary simulation, like the worker pouring sand instead of lead. Most feedback is by the tutor talking to the trainee, but it may be necessary to devise ways of providing greater accuracy or speed to the feedback by methods like television recording or photography. The most common method for teaching motor skills is the progressive-part method that had its most comprehensive explanation by Douglas Seymour (1966). The task to be undertaken by the trainee is broken down into a series of subroutines. The trainee then practises routine 1, routine 2 and then 1+2. The next step is to practise routine 3, 2+3 and 1+2+3, so that competence is built up progressively by practising a subroutine and then attaching it to the full task, which is constantly being practised with an increasing number of the different components included. The components are only practised separately for short periods before being assimilated, so there is no risk of fragmentary performance.

This only works if the job can be subdivided into components. Where this is not possible, simplification offers an alternative. In this method the task to be performed is kept as a whole, but reduced to its simplest form. Skilled performance is then reached by gradually increasing the complexity of the exercises. An example is the art of candle-making. Fancy candles are made by cutting strips down the side of multi-coloured candle blocks and fashioning the strips into elaborate confections. The candle-maker is trained by starting to make candles with little elaboration and gradually increasing the flights of fancy.

Although this chapter is concerned mainly with motor-skill training, there are some specialized methods of memory training which can be listed here, as well as ways of training for perceptual skill. Both types of ability appear to be increasing in importance in organizational life.

The most familiar way of memorizing is the mnemonic or jingle, wherein a simple formula provides the clue to a more comprehensive set of data. 'ASH' is easier to remember than 'Action on Smoking and Health', 'laser' is much easier to remember than 'light amplification by stimulated emission of radiation' and most people employed in schools will remember how the 'Great Education Reform Bill' of 1988 was reduced to the short-hand of 'GERBIL' in staff-room discussions. If the initial letters are not easily memorable, the mnemonic is replaced by the jingle. The denseness of ROYGBIV has led generations of school children to remember that Richard Of York Gave Battle In Vain as a way of recalling the sequence of colours in the spectrum, and the indifference of science teachers to historical accuracy is shown by the fact that another school of thought uses the jingle, Richard Of York Gained Battles In Vain.

For some tasks the use of rules reduces the volume of material to be memorized. There are many fault-finding rules, for instance, where the repairer is taught to use a systematic series of rules. The stranded motorist who telephones the vehicle rescue service for assistance will probably be asked a first question, 'Have you run out of petrol?' The answer 'Yes' identifies the fault, while 'No' leads to the second question, 'Is there any spark?' so that the engineer who comes to help already has some areas of fault eliminated.

Deduction is a method that puts information into categories so that if something does not fit into one category the trainee then uses deduction to conclude that it must belong in another. At the beginning of this chapter was the example of the office messenger remembering that invoices go to Mr Brown and cheques to Mrs Smith. If there was also a Ms Robinson, who received all sales inquiries, complaints, unsolicited sales promotion material, tax returns, questionnaires, applications for employment and so on, the messenger would not need to remember what did go to Ms Robinson, but what did not: invoices to Mr Brown, cheques to Mrs Smith and everything else to Ms Robinson. Some interesting examples of using deduction in training are to be found in Belbin and Downs (1966).

For memorization of information the cumulative-part method is slightly, but significantly, different from the progressive-part method already described, in that the trainee constantly practises the whole task, with each practice session adding an extra component. This is distinct from progressive part in which components are practised separately before being built into the whole. This can be especially useful if the more difficult material is covered first, as it will then get much more rehearsal than that coming later.

A method for the development of perceptual skills is discrimination, which requires the trainee to distinguish between items that appear similar to the untrained eye or ear, nose or fingertip. In a rough-and-ready way it is the procedure followed by the birdwatcher or the connoisseur of wine. First the trainee compares two items which are clearly dissimilar and identifies the points of difference. Then other pairs are produced to be compared, with the differences gradually becoming less obvious. Discrimination can be aided by cueing, which helps the trainee to identify particular features in the early attempts at discrimination by providing arrows or coloured sections. Some people start learning to type with the keys coloured according to whether they should be struck with the left or right hand, or even according to the particular finger which is appropriate. Gradually the cues are phased out as the trainee acquires the competence to identify without them.

Magnification is a way of developing the capacity to distinguish small faults in a process or even small components in machinery. Material for examination is magnified at the beginning of training and then reduced back to normal as competence is acquired. Inspectors of tufted carpet start their training by being shown samples of poor tufting that have been produced using much larger material than normal. Later they examine normal material under a magnifying glass and eventually they are able to examine the normal product. A helpful discussion of magnification method can be found in Holding (1965).

(c) Training programme

The various training methods to be used are put together in a training programme. This sets out not only what the tutor is going to do, but also the progress the trainee is expected to make. Of critical importance here is pacing: how much material the trainee has to take in before practice begins; how long there is to practise before being able to proceed to a new part; and how frequently progress is checked by the tutor. Individual trainees will each have their own rate at which they can proceed and will need differing levels of initial explanation and demonstration before practice can start. Training programmes require sufficient flexibility to accommodate the varying capacities that learners bring to their training.

A useful feature of the training programme is providing scope for trainees to be involved in determining their own rate of progress and some self-discovery, to avoid spoon feeding. At the outset trainees are so conscious of their dependency that all measures that build up confidence, independence and autonomy are welcome.

(d) Selection of trainees

The last feature of preparation is selecting those to be trained. The emphasis will be on basic suitability of individuals for the course that is planned, so that training for a skill requiring deft manipulation will be preceded by selection that establishes either previous success in work involving similar dexterity or potential for such accomplishment that may be determined by aptitude tests. Another consideration is the compatability of trainees who are going to be working together. A tutor providing training on a number of occasions may try to group trainees together with rough similarities of age, experience or aptitude that will make them reasonably similar in the rate at which they are likely to advance.

Encounter

(a) Meeting

When tutor and trainee meet for the first time, there is a mutual appraisal. The process is as described under rapport in Chapter 3, but the 'getting-to-know-you' exchanges are more important than most of the encounters described in this book, as the two people have to work together and the trainee will be uncertain in an unfamiliar situation, and absolutely dependent upon the tutor. Trainees need to feel confidence in the tutor as someone skilled in the task that is to be learned and enthusiastic about teaching it to others. They will also be looking for reassurance about their own chances of success by seeking information about previous trainees.

(b) Explaining procedure

The explanation of procedure will follow as soon as the meeting phase has lasted long enough. Here is the first feature of pacing that was mentioned as part of preparation. There has to be enough time for meeting to do its work, but long, drawn-out introductions can lead to impatience, chafing and wanting to get started.

The procedure is the programme, with the associated details of timing, rate of progress, training methods and the general overview of what is to happen. The most important point to the trainee is obviously the end. When does one 'graduate'? What happens then? Can it be quicker? Do many people fail? What happens to them? The tutor is, of course, more interested in the beginning of the programme rather than the end, but it is only with a clear grasp of the end that the trainee can concentrate on the beginning. Getting the goal clear reinforces the commitment to learning.

With long-running training programmes where an array of skills has to be mastered, the point of graduation may be too distant to provide an effective goal so that the tutor establishes intermediate goals: 'By Friday you will be able to . . . '

This phase benefits from illustration; a timetable, a chart of the average learning curve, samples of work by previous trainees all make more tangible the prospect of success and more complete the mental picture of the operating framework that the trainee is putting together. It is also helpful to avoid the explanation becoming mechanical, like the tourist guide at Windsor Castle. If the tutor has explained the procedure so often that it has become automatic, it is no longer the vivid apotheosis of skill that was described earlier. It is a time for as much interchange as possible, with questions, reiteration, further explanation, clarification and confirmation.

(c) Presenting the task

The task that the trainee has to perform first is demonstrated and explained. The purpose is not to display the tutor's advanced skills, but to provide a basis for the trainee's first, tentative (and possibly incorrect) attempts. The demonstration is thus done without any flourishes or extras, and as slowly as possible, because the tutor is not only demonstrating skill but also using skill to convince the trainees that they can do the job. Accompanying the demonstration, the explanation gives reasons for the different actions being used and describes what is being done so that trainees can watch analytically. Their attention is drawn to features they might overlook, the sequence of actions is recounted and key points are mentioned.

The task must be presented to the trainee in its simplest possible form, with a straightforward, unfussy, accurate demonstration accompanied by an explanation which emphasizes correct sequence, reasons why, features that might be overlooked in the demonstration and the key points that lead to success. Where possible, the tutor should not mention what not to do. Incorrect aspects of performance can be dealt with later, at this stage the direction should be on what to do.

The presentation is followed, and perhaps interrupted, by questions from the trainees on what they did not follow or cannot remember. The success of this will depend on the skill of the tutor in going through the opening stages of the encounter. Many trainees are reluctant to question because they feel that the question reveals their ignorance, which will be judged as stupidity. The experienced tutor can stimulate the questioning and confirming by the trainees through putting questions to them. This is effective only when done well, as there is the obvious risk of inhibiting people by confronting them with their lack of understanding. The most unfortunate type of questions are those which cross-examine:

- 'Now, tell me the three main functions of this apparatus.'
- 'Can anyone remember which switch we press first?'

Little better are the vague requests for assent:

- 'Do you understand?'
- 'Am I making myself clear?'
- 'Is that all right, everybody?'

These are like the leading questions we looked at in Chapter 3. They will be some use as there will be nods and grunts from the trainees to provide response, but it is most unlikely that people will do more than offer the easy, regular 'yes'. The job of the tutor is to help trainees build the picture in their own minds without the feeling that they are being tested. This will only come with good rapport.

(d) Practice

After the presentation the trainees have their first attempt at the task. They expect to do badly, and need confidence from the tutor, who has to steer a difficult path between too much or too little intervention. Too much and the trainees do not 'feel their feet' and acquire the confidence that comes from sensing the strength and purpose of your own first faltering steps. Too little intervention means that trainees learn about their lack of competence, which is reinforced by a performance which falls short of what presentation had suggested as being possible. This shows the importance again of presentation, which has to be pitched at the level that will make initial performance feasible, without building up expectations that cannot be realized.

Among the considerations for tutors are the varying potential of individual trainees and the ritual elements of training. Some trainees will be able to make initial progress much more rapidly than others, so that pegging all to the same rate of advance will inhibit both. The ritual features depend on the acknowledgement by the trainee of the absolute, albeit temporary, superiority of the tutor. It has already been pointed out that there is a reluctance to question during presentation; there are also intermittent displays of deference to the tutor. This enables trainees to perform badly during practice without losing face. However, deference to a superior figure is normally offered on the assumption that the novice is being helped towards the advanced state of grace that the superior enjoys. If early practice of a taught skill produces abject performances by the trainees, then they either lose confidence or resent the instructor for highlighting the trainee's inadequacy.

Learning theory tells us the importance of the law of effect, which practice makes possible, but it also tells us that there is likely to be a point at which the trainee makes a sudden leap forward – the point at which the penny drops and there is a shared excitement. In the words of Professor Higgins about Eliza: 'I think she's got it. By Jove, she's got it.' Practice leads up to the point where the learning spurts forward and it then provides the reinforcement of that learning by continued rehearsal and confirmation.

(e) Reinforcement

The most effective reinforcement for trainees is realizing that they can perform, like the child who at last finds it possible to remain erect and mobile on a bicycle. Trainees cannot usually rely on their own interpretation of success: they will need constant assessment by the tutor. Many of the text books on teaching and learning emphasize the value of praise, a little of which apparently goes a long way, for example:

> When they are learning people need to know where they stand, they need to know how they are progressing. The knowledge of their progress spurs them on to greater achievements. In this respect praise is always far more helpful than criticism. (Winfield, 1979, p. 81)

Effective reinforcement enables trainees to understand both the result and the actions or behaviour which produced the result, so the tutor needs to identify the particular ways in which progress is being made and explain their merit, as well as explaining what caused the progress to happen. When trainees are approaching full competence, with the associated self-confidence, then they are able to cope with more direct criticism.

Follow-up

(a) Integration

The first follow-up step to a training episode is when trainees integrate their new learning with their existing store of knowledge, understanding and skill so as to extend their overall performance potential. This may be done by the trainee alone, but more probably with the tutor. The new facet of skill is placed in a number of different contexts so that what has been learned makes possible a whole range of new possibilities. Once an apprentice has learned to plane the edge of a piece of wood smooth, that ability, of itself valueless, is made valuable by being able to combine it with other routines. The sequence of explanation, demonstration and practice begins once more.

(b) Evaluation

Evaluating the effectiveness of the training episode will increase the tutor's store of knowledge for dealing with future trainees. Simple methods are the most reliable, like records of the time taken to reach the different levels of effectiveness. Further suggestions about evaluation are to be found in Harrison (1988)

(c) Checking progress and coaching

When training is complete, the role of the manager in relation to the trainee changes. Now it is necessary to spot aspects of slack practice that are beginning to develop or help with overcoming a temporary problem. This is not an easy role, as the trainee may not welcome the errors of inexperience being pointed out, but it remains a necessary aspect of follow-up.

(d) Changing methods

The manager will regularly consider changes and improvements to training methods that are used. Although on-going, such possibilities of change are easiest to see when an episode of training has been completed.

Table 7.1 *The training for skill sequence*

Preparation
1. Review:
   - training objectives.
2. Select:
   - learning methods;
   - progressive-part method;
   - simplification;
   - mnemonics or jingles;
   - rules;
   - deduction;
   - cumulative part;
   - discrimination;
   - magnification.
3. Compile:
   - training programme.
4. Select:
   - trainees.

Encounter
1. Meet for:
   - mutual appraisal.
2. Explain:
   - procedure.
3. Present:
   - task.
4. Allow:
   - trainee to practise.
5. Reinforce:
   - performance.

Follow-up
1. Integrate:
   - new learning with existing knowledge.
2. Evaluate:
   - training effectiveness.
3. Check:
   - progress, and coach.
4. Change:
   - methods, where necessary.

References

Belbin, E. and R. M. Belbin, (1972) *Problems in Adult Retraining*, Heinemann, London.

Belbin, E. and S. Downs, (1966) 'Teaching and paired associates', *Journal of Occupational Psychology*, 40, 67–74.

Fitts, P. M. and M. J. Posner (1967) *Human Performance*, Brooks Cole, Belmont, CA.

Harrison, R. (1988) *Training and Development*, Institute of Personnel Management, London.

Holding, D. H. (1965) *Principles of Training: Research in applied learning*, Pergamon, Oxford.

ITRU (Industrial Training Research Unit) (1976) *Choose an Effective Style: A self-instructional approach to the teaching of skills*, ITRU Publications, Cambridge.

Rushby, N. (ed.) (1987) *Technology-based Learning: Selected readings*, Kogan Page, London.

Seymour, W. D. (1966) *Industrial Skills*, Pitman, London.

Winfield, I. (1979) *Learning to Teach Practical Skills*, Kogan Page, London.

Exercise 7

Devise a training programme that will teach someone to complete a straightforward task, taking care to go through all the steps of preparation that have been mentioned in this chapter. Then teach someone to complete the task.

Some of the tasks you could consider are the following:

1. Folding a table napkin.
2. Laying out a tray to serve someone a full English breakfast in bed.
3. Doing a conjuring trick.
4. Executing a waterfall shuffle with playing cards.
5. Making a cake.
6. Packing a collection of tinned food in a box.
7. Laying out a tray, as in 2 above, but for someone who is left-handed.

8 Putting it over: Making a speech or presentation

Speaking to an audience has been one of the ways in which people have achieved power and influence over others, partly because of the importance of their message and partly because of the emotional power of their delivery of that message. It has been an assertion of leadership and symbolic of authority. In the careers of charismatic leaders significant stages are often highlighted by speeches: Paul of Tarsus on the Areopagus in Athens, Henry V rallying his troops before Agincourt, Lincoln at Gettysburg and Churchill during the Battle of Britain are all examples. The most extreme instance of such influence was probably Adolf Hitler:

> Speech was an essential medium of his power, not only over his audiences but over his own temperament. Hitler talked incessantly, often using words less to communicate his thoughts than to release the hidden spring of his own and others' emotions, whipping himself and his audience into anger or exaltation by the sound of his voice. (Bullock, 1969)

There is little scope for this type of oratory in organizational life, though there are frequent attempts by individual managers to incorporate aspects of propaganda into addresses they make to groups of employees in an attempt to change their attitudes and behaviour.

More common in working life are addresses intended to increase the knowledge and understanding of audience members, such as on a training course or at a sales presentation. This is where few are effective and many are frightened. It is the widespread fear of speaking in public that gives such power to those who seem to have conquered the fear. Considerable self-confidence comes to those who can cope with something that daunts most people they know. Too many managers regard speaking in public as something beyond them:

Many managers, both male and female, suffer from the delusion that speaking in public is the same as a theatrical performance, or something suitable only for extroverts. This delusion often serves as a defence. The plain truth is that they fear exposure of their limitations as speakers . . . .If a man has something worth saying, he should not only say it but also learn to say it will full effect. (Bell, 1989, p. 46)

As was shown in the telecommunication analogy, success in putting it over lies in getting the message received and understood: not in transmitting it. There may be many different receivers, all of whom have to be kept switched on and tuned in by the speaker. In selection, counselling, market research and discipline there is only one receiver; in training there will seldom be more than five or six; and arbitration and negotiation also involve only small groups. Speaking to an audience will usually involve dozens or hundreds of receivers. Another important difference between this interaction and others is the length of transmission. There is not the scope for two-way traffic that there is in the other situations, yet the multitude of receivers will all be operating at varying levels of efficiency. Some will be working efficiently while others are switched to another channel. Some will be producing one decoding of the message while others are producing another. It would be unduly optimistic to say that the speaker should get all the receivers working on the same wavelength in the same way.

This can be illustrated by examples from entertainment. As the performance at a pop concert becomes more frenzied and libidinous nearly all members of the audience will combine in a united response, with postural echoes, hands high above heads, glazed expressions and general ecstasy. Some, however, will react quite differently, sitting silent or inattentive. Even the comedian, getting a steadily rising level of laughter from the audience with every succeeding joke, will never make all the audience laugh.

The speaker in the lecture room, at the shareholders' meeting or at the sales conference will never get everyone's attention, but still needs to win over as many members of the audience as possible. As with other performances, there is scope for preparation, rehearsal and careful manipulation of the physical environment to achieve the maximum effect. This is why there is more emphasis on preparation in this chapter than in any of the others.

The speech or presentation sequence

Preparation

(a) The status of the speaker

Is the speaker the right person to deliver this message to this audience? The audience will turn up their receivers if the speaker has prestige; if not, they will turn off or even not tune in. The main determinant of appropriateness to deliver a message is the credence the audience gives to the speaker's standing and expertise. If they see the speaker as a person with information that will be of use to them, then they will accord the necessary status and listen. If the ensuing presentation disappoints them they will not only become inattentive, they are likely to signal their disillusion with demoralizing clarity. Audiences show little compunction about humiliating speakers, who assume authority with all its ritual trappings, such as standing while the audience sits, occupying special, distant space and anticipating their attention.

Another aspect of status is hierarchical. Senior members of organizations are expected to speak on important matters ('We want it from the horse's mouth'). When the level of the message does not match the level of the speaker then there will be mistrust. Here are two actual examples. A general manager called all the shop stewards together simply to announce that the toilet doors were to be painted white; the members of the audience dispersed asking each other what he really meant. A lowly-placed charge-hand announced that the factory was to be closed; the audience would not believe him and demanded corroboration. The small exception to this is the way in which those with power can invest it in their close aides, like the Buckingham Palace spokesman. In informal situations, at least, private secretaries and personal assistants to managing directors speak with considerable authority.

(b) The room

The arrangements of the room improve the quality of the presentation. Referring to the manipulation of space, described in Chapter 2, the distance between the speaker and the audience will usually be that of the public zone. The speaker will use eye contact with the audience as a means of control and this is made difficult if anyone is too close. The seating is best arranged so that there are approximately the right number of seats. Too many will tend to scatter the members of the audience, making it harder for the speaker to get them to behave like an audience rather than a collection of individuals.

The position from which to speak is dictated by the arrangements for the audience, but problems that typically curse unprepared speakers are a lack of anywhere to put notes, a distracting background behind the speaker, problems with microphones or some problem with visual aids. Visual aids are referred to shortly, but the problem of the distracting background is not always appreciated (Figure 8.1). The audience needs to look at the speaker so as to concentrate on what they are hearing. Visual aids should embellish

Figure 8.1 *The problem of the distracting background is not always appreciated*

the presentation; other visual images will be a distraction. Examples are murals, stained-glass windows, blackboards that are not being used or charts on the wall. Speakers who scorn the blackboard because they have a sheaf of acetate sheets to show on the overhead projector often overlook the fact that members of the audience will tend to read what is on the blackboard, even though it was written by someone else the day before.

One large company has a lecture room in its training centre that is used for management-training sessions. On the wall to one side of the speaker's position is a wall chart of the periodic table of chemical elements. During any session all members of an audience spend some time examining the chart, whether they be chemists making sure they can remember the sequence or non-chemists trying to understand it.

(c) The material
What is to be said or, more accurately, what should members of the audience go away having understood and remembered? The starting point is a plan with the three elements of introduction, substance and conclusion.

In the introduction the speaker sets up rapport with the audience. Apart from their attention the speaker will include here an answer to the unspoken question – is it going to be worth our while listening? A useful introduction is to explain what the members of the audience will know or be able to do at the end. It is also helpful to sketch out the framework of what is to come, so that people can follow it more readily. But stick to what you promise. If you say there are going to be five points, the audience will listen for five to make sure that they have not missed one. In the substance is the message that is to be conveyed, the development of the argument and the build-up of what it is that the audience should go away having understood and remembered. The conclusion is where the main points of the substance are reiterated and confirmed in a brief, integrated summary.

In the substance there will be a number of key thoughts or ideas. This is what the speaker is trying to plant in the minds of the audience: not facts, which are inert, but the ideas which facts may well illustrate and clarify. The idea that inflation is dangerously high is only illustrated by the fact that it is at a particular figure in a particular month.

The ideas in an exposition can be helpfully linked together by a device that will help audience members to remember them and to grasp their interdependence. One method is to enshrine the ideas in a story. If the story is recalled the thoughts are recalled with it, as they are integral to the structure. The classic examples of this are the New Testament parables, but every play, novel or film uses the same method. Another method is to use key words to identify the points that are being made, especially if they have an alliterative or mnemonic feature, like 'Planning Progress and Prosperity'. In a lecture it is common to provide a framework for ideas by using a drawing or system model to show the interconnection of points.

Facts, by giving impact, keep together the framework of ideas that the speaker has assembled. They clarify and give dimension to what is being said. The danger is to use too many, so that the audience are overwhelmed by facts and figures which begin to bemuse them.

Humour is the most dangerous of all aids to the speaker. If the audience laughs at a funny story, it will be encouraging and may relieve any tension that may be present, but how tempting to try again and end up 'playing for laughs'. Laughter is a most seductive human reaction, but too many laughs are even more dangerous than too many facts. What will the audience remember – the joke, or what the joke was to illustrate? Attempted humour is also dangerous for the ineffective comedian. If you tell what you think is a funny story and no-one laughs, you have made a fool of yourself (at least in your own eyes) and risk floundering.

Very few people speak effectively without notes, despite the tendency to marvel at those who can. Relying solely on memory risks missing something out, getting a fact wrong or drying up completely. Notes provide discipline and limit the tendency to ramble. How irritating it is for members of an audience to maintain attention when the speaker 'pauses for a moment to mention in passing' something that interferes with their attempt to keep hold on their own mental picture of the address.

There are two basic kinds of notes: headlines or a script. Headlines are probably the most common, with main points underlined and facts listed beneath. Sometimes there will also be a marginal note about an anecdote or other type of illustration. Table 8.1 is an example taken from the notes of a sales manager addressing a sales conference.

The alternative of the script enables the speaker to try out the exact wording, phrases and pauses to achieve the greatest effect. The script will benefit from some marking or arrangement that will help you to find your place again as your eyes constantly flick from the page to

Table 8.1 *Notes: Headlines*

Points	Facts				Quotes, etc.
1. Our market share has declined over the last year.	Period	Us	Co.A	Others	(a) Comment by JB at advertising agency.
	J–M	27%	22%	51%	(b) Story from customer Z.
	A–J	24%	26%	50%	
	J–S	25%	25%	50%	
	O–D	22%	27%	51%	
2. Not due to production difficulties.	(a) No stoppages in period. (b) Production has risen 3%. (c) Customer complaints on quality down.				Questions from works convener at production committee.

the audience and back again. This can be underlining or using a highlighter. Another method of organizing a script is to use a form of blank verse. The best-known user of this method was Winston Churchill, but Peter Marshall, the Scottish-born Chaplain of the United States at the end of the Second World War, used a similar method for sermon notes. Table 8.2 shows how this method not only helped him find his place, but also gave cues for pauses and emphasis.

Table 8.2 *Notes: Script* (Source: Marshall, 1954, p. 51)

It is not easy to live out your life day after day
and week after week
and year after year in a subordinate position,
while somebody else gets the notice
the publicity
the attention
the credit
the praise
the spotlight
and perhaps the reward

(d) The speaker
The final feature of preparation is of the speaker, who has to bring the notes to life. Rehearsal can help eliminate potential difficulties but it depends on a third party to listen and comment on what is being said. Only in this way will there be an indication of what is heard and understood, as well as what is being said. So the first rehearsal check is on the clarity of expression; the second is on audibility. Occasional speakers find it difficult to speak loud enough to be heard at the same time as speaking naturally. Also there is a strange tendency to drop the voice at the end of sentences, losing the last few words.

Few people avoid stage fright. To some extent this is useful, as it keys up the speaker to produce a vivid performance. Too much stage fright, however, can destroy it. Confidence is essential in getting the audience to listen. Diffidence and nervousness may be engaging qualities in athletes who have just broken a world record or in bridegrooms at wedding receptions, but not for business speakers. It can be reduced by deliberate relaxation, moving consciously a little more slowly than usual and concentrating on the deliberate relaxation of different muscles. Much can be achieved by breathing exercises, as advocated by Winifred Marks:

> It is relaxing simply to take several long, deep breaths, filling the base of the lungs and activating the diaphragm. More sophisticated techniques have been advocated, such as holding the nose between thumb and middle finger, with the index finger on the bridge and pressing the nostrils in turn to enforce breathing through each one alternately. (Marks, 1980, p. 51)

A less complicated method is to breathe in to a steady count of three and out to an equally steady count of nine; in to four and out to twelve; in to five and out to fifteen and so on. Marks also makes the interesting suggestion that speakers should smile as much as possible before starting, as this will remove traces of an anxious frown and relax facial muscles before confronting the audience.

Encounter

Now begins the experience that some people find more frightening than any other: facing the audience. Sometimes the result can be exhilarating; all too frequently it is humiliating. The ritual is of one person asserting authority over others and the speaker cannot avoid that role. Disclaimers, apologies and appeals to the better nature of the audience are of no use, as the only reason for the event is that the speaker has some authority that members of the audience respect, and that is the expectation to which you have to rise. The audience that is satisfied will 'applaud' and flatter you in a dozen ways: the dissatisfied audience is merciless.

(a) Rapport
Rapport and its development has many features. Appearance is particularly important, not in the sense of best suits or polished shoes, but what the appearance of the speaker says to the audience. The way we present ourselves to others says something of our attitude towards them – we have taken trouble to get ready, or we have not. This may be regarded as the trivia of manners, but virtually everyone works on their appearance to create an effect. An audience will scrutinize your appearance closely, as they are trapped, with very little else to look at. Do you look prepared and organized? Do you look as if you care what they think? Appearance can also distract. How much further is that zip going to slide in the next twenty minutes? I wonder where she got those earrings? I'm sure he's got odd socks on. That bracelet must have cost a fortune.

Stance is an expression of authority: you stand, they have to sit. It is not always essential to stand, as the organization of the room will probably give you enough special space to maintain your authority while sitting, but you deny yourself the chance for building up initial confidence slightly if you do not take this opportunity. The speaker's confident manner can make the audience believe that it is all going to be worthwhile. It is not enough, but it helps.

The speaker will also demonstrate and foster contact with the audience and involvement with them. One way is to explain the structure of the presentation, the reasons for it, why the exponent is the person doing it and what the outcome could be for the audience. You need to avoid the risk of creating false hopes, as it is pointless to generate a positive response at the beginning which is let down by what follows, so that the audience leaves disgruntled.

The best method of contact is to look at the audience. This is difficult for inexperienced speakers, who regard the audience as a Hydra-headed monster and dare not look it in the eye, preferring to gaze intently either at their notes, a spot on the floor six inches in front of their feet or the top right-hand corner of the ceiling. Such faint hearts should remember a figure from Greek mythology – the Gorgon, one glance from whom turned the observer to stone. The roles of speaker and listener are so clearly dominant and submissive that people in the audience who see the speaker looking at them will appear interested, stop yawning, sit up straight, stop talking, defer the crossword till later or whatever other behaviour is consistent with being observed by an authority figure.

Mayerson suggests that there are three significant non-verbal cues that the speaker gives to affect audience response. The first is energy level (Figure 8.2):

> If he looks as if he needs a lectern to prop him up, he conveys a low energy level. If he seems bursting with vigor, he conveys a high energy level. The freedom with which he turns his head, smiles and moves his hands, the control of the breath as he sends forth his words, his speech volume, his articulation, and his spacing and pausing all contribute to an image of energy level. (Mayerson, 1979, p. 183)

Second is flexibility of movement and third comes the speaker's warmth and enthusiasm:

> Enthusiasm is contagious. If a speaker wants to convince, he has to believe in the issue himself. His belief helps to get the message across. There is a difference between 'We have to do something

Figure 8.2 *If the lecturer needs the lectern to prop himself up, he conveys a low evergy level*

about wasted materials' said as the speaker picks lint off his trousers, scans the horizon, stifles a yawn, or scratches his head, and 'We have to do something about wasted materials' said with inflection, pausing, direct eye contact and an erect posture. (Mayerson, 1979, p. 184)

Try some other line of business if you have planned to start by saying, 'My wife (husband, brother, mother, sister) said I should stop boring if I did not strike oil in the first fifteen minutes.'

(b) Development

After the audience has been won over – and even if it has not! – the speaker moves on to develop the argument. The form of development is predetermined by the preparation that has been made: the number of ideas, the relevant facts, the illustrations and so on. It is now that the value of that preparation is felt. Do not, however, fall into the trap of thinking that your opening funny story, with eye contact and a list of points to be covered is all the 'performance' that is required. Audience attention and involvement has to be sustained through the manner of the exposition:

interest and motivation should be sustained throughout by the use of material or examples which are intrinsically interesting to the audience, dramatic, or simply funny. Concrete examples and stories make the material easier to assimilate, and should be subordinated to the main argument. (Argyle, 1972, p. 209)

(c) Voice

The voice is the means by which the material is transmitted and has to be loud and clear to be effective. The two most common problems about audibility are not being heard at the back of the room and not being heard at the end of sentences. Being heard at the back can be overcome by speaking to the back row and using eye contact to pick up the signals from those members of the audience sitting there. When they lean forward, cupping a hand to an ear or shake their heads at each other in bewilderment, you have a clear signal that there are problems requiring an increase in volume. The back row is also usually populated by awkward members of the audience; those anxious to slip out before the end and those least interested in the subject matter. Some hard-bitten exponents – like bishops and head-masters – deploy the tactic of an opening question, 'Can you hear me at the back?' delivered in a vigorous bellow to produce a whispered, 'Yes', which is then followed by, 'As soon as you can't hear, put a hand up or something.' The members of the back row have then been stripped of the comfortable obscurity they were seeking and spend the rest of the exposition sitting nervously on the edges of their seats in case they are asked another question.

All speakers seem to have a natural tendency for volume to drop at the end of sentences, partly because they are running out of breath. In trying to overcome this difficulty there is the risk of becoming monotonous, as everything is on the same level, without any appropriate reference to the meaning of the words being spoken. Pace in speaking probably needs to be slowed down, as that of normal conversation is too quick for talking to a large audience of receivers. Also the speaking goes on for a much longer period without interruption, so that the speaker needs a slower pace to permit breathing and thinking. There is still the need to vary pace to provide selective emphasis.

There is also scope for pauses, to enable breathing and emphasis and to help audience comprehension. They also help to eliminate the nonsense words that frequently occur as someone is speaking:

A recent gathering of mature men and women were listening for sixty minutes to a distinguished academic. Within fifteen minutes of him starting to talk, several members of the audience had stopped listening so that they could concentrate on the frequency with which he used the phrases 'in fact' and 'as it were'. Subsequent comparison of findings showed that the rate was once every sixteen seconds and once every forty-seven seconds respectively. (Torrington, 1972, p. 87)

Other examples are 'right', 'OK' and 'you know'. The reason for this type of distracting interjection is that the flow of ideas and the operation of the tongue are not correctly synchronized, so that meaningless words and sounds are produced occasionally to fill the void that the brain has momentarily left. Practice can replace nonsense words with pauses, which are better for the audience and for the exponent.

(d) Language

Language needs to be what the audience will understand. The larger and more heterogeneous the audience, the more difficult for the speaker to cover that wide range of capacities. Marks (1980, pp. 54–60) has some helpful advice on this and points out how easy it is for professionals to slip into jargon that can puzzle many people, like the marketing manager to whom everything is a mix and the industrial relations manager to whom everything is a package. Few things can antagonize an audience more than the feeling that the speaker is trying to impress them with cleverness rather than putting the message over.

(e) Closing

At the end the speaker summarizes the points that have been made, reinforces them and leads the audience to some sort of follow-up action. That action may often be no more than to remember something of what has been heard, or to feel reassured, but it is the closing that will lead to the action. The speaker has to avoid an anti-climax, which can be caused by signalling the end too clearly: 'Let me sum up what I have been trying to say . . . ' That both indicates that there is nothing new and confirms the view of the audience that it has not been well done. Instead the exponent aims for a climax – a positive close. Among the ways to do this are telling a story, which brings together and illustrates the points that have been made; raising rhetorical questions to which members of the audience can now see answers where they could not at the beginning; and a straightforward statement which shows the inter-relationship of points made earlier.

(f) Pitfalls

The inexperienced speaker should guard against some of the more common pitfalls, one of which is apology. If members of the audience are disciplining themselves to sit still and listen it will not make them more responsive if you tell them of your incompetence. Your best hope is to try and conceal it, rather than emphasizing it. Shortly after a serious airport disaster, a fire officer addressed a press conference with the opening, 'I cannot promise you that I have expert knowledge on this subject, so perhaps I may share with you some of my own confusion.'

All of us can recall situations in which a speaker's mannerisms distracted us from what was being said (Figure 8.3). They are a form of displacement activity and should not be restrained to the point of making the presentation wooden or stilted, but can be modified to avoid too much distraction. A common mannerism is walking about. In moderation, this provides a mild variation in scene, but some of the more distracting variations are the walks that follow a precise, oft-repeated path to and fro, or those which include little flourishes like a slow motion, modified goose step. Standing still can be little better if it is accompanied by the act of balancing on the outside edges of one's shoes or using a toe to sketch, with great care and precision, a cross or triangle in the imaginary dust on the floor.

Figure 8.3 *A speaker's mannerisms can distract from what is being said*

Some people reserve for their public speeches a minute examination of their fingernails or a series of isometric exercises to relieve muscular aches in their shoulders. Rings and bracelets are frequently played with incessantly, but the greatest distractor of all is probably the pair of spectacles that goes on, comes off, gets folded and put away, only to be taken out, unfolded, put on and so on.

Some speakers lose their audience by not stopping when they have finished, rambling from one anti-climactic afterthought to another as the audience chafes because the coffee will be getting cold. When you have said, 'And finally . . . ' you have no more than two minutes left. If you follow this with 'To conclude . . .', and later, 'As a last word . . .' and later still 'And this really is my last word . . .', you may excite sufficient wrath in the audience for them to start throwing things.

(g) Visual aids

We remember what we see for longer than we remember what we are told, and we can sometimes understand what we see better than we can understand what we hear. This is the rationale for the use of blackboards, overhead projectors, films, television, working models and experiments. They are, however, aids to, and not substitutes for, the presentation. Too much displayed material can obscure rather than illuminate what is being said. Television news provides a good example of how much can be used. The dominant theme is always the talking head with frequently intercut pieces of film. Very seldom do words appear on the screen and then usually as extracts from a speech or report, where a short sentence or passage is regarded as being especially meaningful. The other way in which words and numbers appear is when facts are needed to illustrate an idea, so that ideas like football scores or like a change in the value of the pound sterling almost always have the figures shown on the screen to clarify and illustrate. Seldom, however, will more than two or three numbers be displayed at the same time.

Speakers need to remember the size of what they are displaying as well as its complexity. Material has to be big enough for people to read and simple enough for them to follow. Material also has to be timed to coincide with what is being said. Where an exponent is using a display with quite a lot of information, it may be sensible to mask it and reveal one section at a time as the exposition proceeds, so that some members do not move on to a part of the diagram or table that has not yet been explained and which they do not yet understand.

Table 8.3 *The speech or presentation sequence*

Preparation
1. Review:
   - status of the speaker;
   - the room:
     o seating and distance;
     o visual aids (size and complexity);
     o visual distractions;

2. Plan the material:
   - introduction and rapport;
   - substance:
     o key thoughts or ideas;
     o facts;
     o humour;
     o notes: headlines or script.

3. Prepare yourself:
   - by rehearsal;
   - avoid stagefright.

Encounter
1. Check:
   - appearance;
   - stance;
   - contact with the audience:
     o energy level;
     o flexibility of movement;
     o warmth and enthusiasm.

2. Develop with:
   - loud and clear voice;
   - pace;
   - pauses;
   - understandable language.

3. Close.

4. Avoid the pitfalls of:
   - apology;
   - mannerisms;
   - not stopping.

Follow-up
   - Hand-outs.
   - Measurement of understanding.
   - Further meetings.

Follow-up

The objective of follow-up is to reinforce the understanding that the members of the audience have developed through the presentation.

(a) Hand-outs

A typed synopsis of what has been said, or a copy of a diagram that has been displayed, can be helpful in reinforcement, but may reduce the level of concentration during the presentation itself. Furthermore, some members of the audience will not read through the notes because they have just listened to what they contain.

(b) Measurement of understanding

For some presentations, like those used on induction courses, there is scope for checking understanding by the audience through using a questionnaire to test recollection of main points, but this is a rather threatening operation.

(c) Further meetings

If the exposition is one in a series of lectures, number two can reinforce number one by starting with linking material and continuing with occasional references back to earlier coverage. Another way of using further meetings for reinforcement is if small discussion groups are run, so that points can be picked up, clarified and developed further. This is the principle of briefing groups as well as the seminar in education.

References

Argyle, M. (1972) *The Psychology of Interpersonal Behaviour*, Pelican, Harmondsworth, Middlesex.

Bell, G. (1989) *Speaking and Business Presentations*, Heinemann, London.

Bullock, A. (1969) *Hitler: A study in tyranny*, Penguin, London.

Marks, W. (1980) *How to Give a Speech*, IPM, London.

Marshall, P. (1954) *Mr. Jones, Meet the Master*, Peter Davies, London.

Mayerson, E. W. (1979) *Shoptalk*, Saunders, Philadelphia.

Torrington, D. P. (1972) *Face to Face*, Gower, London.

Exercise 8

1. The next time you attend a presentation or listen to a speech given by someone else, study the arrangement of the room and note the changes that you would (and could) make if you were the speaker.

2. Obtain from your library a book or audio cassette of speeches made by an effective orator – such as Winston Churchill, Billy Graham, John Kennedy or Martin Luther King – and make notes of the plan of their material.

3. Prepare a five minute speech on one of these topics:
   (a) walking;
   (b) gardening;
   (c) your favourite sport;
   (d) your hobby;
   (e) your first boyfriend/girlfriend.

   After careful preparation, deliver the speech in an empty room (the garage would do) and record it. Play it back several times, making critical notes of energy level, voice, pace, pauses, etc., following the points in the chapter, then deliver the speech again whilst making a recording.

   - In what ways is it better?
   - In what ways not as good?
   - What have you learned about the way you speak?
   - What can you still improve?

   If you can move on to video-recording, the benefits of the exercises are greater, but it is wise to start with audio recording only and probably better not to video-record for a wider audience than yourself. Group discussion of video-recorded presentations can be very inhibiting.

9 Putting it over: Selling

The popular view is that face-to-face selling is not a respectable occupation. Books, films and television always portray a salesman (rarely in fiction a saleswoman) either as a shabby, middle-aged 'commercial traveller' sitting morosely alongside a half pint of mild in the saloon bar, or as a pushy young 'smartypants' who dresses a little too well and has a smooth line of talk that persuades decent folk to buy things they do not want. The ultimate condemnation was the famous line about American President Richard Nixon, 'Would you buy a used car from this man?' The purpose of that comment was to make a fool of Richard Nixon, but it also classified those who sell as untrustworthy tricksters who never have your own interests at heart.

It is the element of one-to-one persuasion that makes us uneasy. Politicians try to persuade us, but it is not usually one-to-one and politics is a public business with someone else readily available to contradict the line of argument. Advertising sets out to persuade us, but that does not worry us, because it seems impersonal and we have complete control over when to switch off, turn over or throw into the waste paper basket. The sales representative, however, is there at the office door or on the doorstep and makes us feel trapped.

This unease on the part of the customer has led to selling being euphemized into something else. Those who sell usually have a title that uses 'sales' as an adjective in front of a reassuring, respectable noun: sales agent, sales consultant, sales director, sales engineer, sales executive, sales leader, sales manager, sales officer, sales representative. Sometimes the euphemism is developed by adding an extra adjective at the beginning, such as 'area', 'commercial', 'district', 'industrial', 'professional', 'regional', 'senior', 'technical', without these words being taken literally. 'Senior technical sales consultant', for instance, sounds an odd title for the eighteen-year-old who knocks on your door to ask if you would like someone else to call with a quotation for double-glazing the house.

Running alongside this popular view of selling as something that is done to you against your will, there is the increasing emphasis on the marketing orientation of business and attempts to involve all employees in customer care. There is also the modern phenomenon of shopping as a leisure pursuit. Instead of couples despatching their grumpy adolescent children to the grocer's with a shopping list, they drive to the shopping precinct to stroll round the malls while being lulled by the muzak. They probably call in at the coffee shop before wheeling their trolley into the hypermarket. The functional purpose of buying things you need is wrapped up into an allegedly pleasurable activity served up by cohorts of sales assistants who insist on being polite because they are trained to respond pleasantly even when you vent upon them your pent-up frustrations after losing a skirmish with another trolley.

We quite like sales assistants because they assist rather than sell. We do not like sales executives, representatives and so forth because they take charge; they invade; they push and we seldom realize how fragile all their fluent self-confidence really is. But selling must go on if we want to expand our experiences and extend our material possessions. New areas of tourism are opened up because they are sold to potential travellers. People invest their savings in unit trusts instead of putting it all in a sock under the bed because the idea is sold to them. All the new things we come to enjoy have to be sold to us to overcome our inertia.

The popular mistrust of sales people gives them problems too. They need to develop assertiveness and bolster their self-confidence because our response to their professional need to push is often aggressive, resentful and downright rude.

If you are to sell, you first have to decide that you are the sales type. There is a risk of suggesting that the stereotypes described at the beginning of the chapter are correct and that you have to be born with a gift for selling. Although that would be misleading, selling is an activity for which some people appear quite unsuited, and type of personality is more important for selling than for most of the other types of situation described in this book.

Firstly, it is necessary to be the sort of person who is responsive to other people. One of the standard methods psychologists use to classify people is to place them between the extremes of introversion – directing interest inward towards one's own thoughts and feelings rather than towards the external world or making social contacts – or extroversion, more concerned with external reality than with inner feelings. On this classification sales people are more likely to be extrovert than introvert; but we must remember that we are not one or the other; we are somewhere between the two extremes.

In selling, you have to be constantly alert to the other person, listening for cues, sensing interest or disinterest and shaping your sales presentation to the buyer's potential to buy. There are probably more people who have selling potential than those who have not, so hee are a few identifiers. If you answer yes to any of these, think again:

- Do you know what you want to say and then go ahead and say it, finding interruptions disconcerting because they throw you off course and you have to back track in order to pick up the threads of what you were trying to say?

- Do you find there are a lot of people you meet who irritate you because they do not understand, are slow to pick up new ideas or seem full of their own importance?

- Do you have a small number of friends or acquaintances with very similar interests to yourself and no real desire to increase the number and variety of your acquaintances?

- Do you feel ill at ease among people you do not know well?

It is also important to be someone who finds it easy to be positive and confident; selling is no life for the lugubrious. You need a positive approach in all sales encounters, no matter what the problems. If you meet a buyer for the first time and begin by agreeing on how absolutely awful the weather is, and what a foul climate we have to live in, and that things will certainly be worse by the week-end, then you have established an atmosphere between you that is negative, looking on the black side, feeling miserable and hopeless, making it easy for the buyer to say 'no'. In contrast, the positive approach can lighten a glum atmosphere and make even the buyer think of opportunities rather than problems. If you are confident as well as positive, the buyer begins to believe in the quality of the product or service you are selling.

The selling approach varies considerably, so the approach in this chapter is a very general view of the face-to-face selling process.

The selling sequence

Preparation

(a) Objectives

Each contact with a customer needs to have specific objectives. A call which is just to keep in touch tends to be a waste of time for both parties. A strategy of trying to obtain an order on every visit is likely to be frustrating and unproductive. The objective-setting approach to selling is based on the simple idea that people work best when they have particular objectives to meet, just as we have seen in Chapter 7 that trainees work best with specified stages to reach after defined periods of time. This is not the same as sales targets, which are usually to be achieved each week, each month or each year. Every sales interview needs an objective, such as the following:

- Delivering a quotation, explaining it and pointing out key features.
- Obtaining information needed to prepare a quotation.
- Introducing a new product or range.
- Providing up-dated information on prices, special promotions, discounts or similar encouragements to buy.
- Dealing with a query or complaint.
- Arranging for the buyer to visit the factory.
- Seeking payment of an overdue account.

(b) Names and information
You never, ever forget the names of your clients and their colleagues It is an old saying in sales that customers like nothing better than hearing their own name. They also like to see it spelt correctly, preferably preceded by all their initials or by their correctly spelt first name. It is also worth trying to get titles right. People who have taken the trouble to obtain the qualification usually appreciate being addressed as Dr, and not all women like the appellation of Ms.

The value of getting names right is not only to flatter the buyer, but also to show that you are well prepared.

Other types of information about the buyer or the company are accumulated by the observant and can help shape the sales presentation, such as news of the company in the national or local press, or new equipment in the factory. There are a number of potential clues about the buyer (Figure 9.1):

- Is there an ash tray with signs of use?
- Is there a family photograph?
- Does the poster from Marbella indicate a recent holiday?
- What items of decoration tell you something about the occupant of the office: trophies, pictures, framed certificates, trade magazines on the desk?

(c) Obtaining the interview
Arranging an interview with a client is made difficult by the defences that clients erect. You are trying – ever so nicely – to push your way in, they are resisting you taking control of their freedom of

" ..... HAVE YOU EVER BEEN TO SPAIN, MR SMITH?"

Figure 9.1 *Potential clues about the buyer*

movement. Commissionaires, telephonists, receptionists, secretaries are all in the way. Calling cold is usually a waste of time and is only used when there is a gap in the selling day that can be filled in by calling on one or two prospective clients 'on spec'. Normally interviews are obtained by telephone.

It is essential to know your prospective client's name and to try and speak to him or her personally. If you succeed in getting through to the client, the objective is to secure a time and date for a meeting, so you have to be prepared, knowing exactly when you could be there. It probably helps to suggest a specific time period: 'Could I call and see you for a few minutes some time on Thursday morning?' is more likely to be successful than either 'I would like to call and see you for a few minutes. When would be convenient?' (which is too vague and easy to avoid) or, 'Could I call and see you for a few minutes at 10.30 on Thursday morning?' (which is too specific a time, allowing the client no choice). You also have to have good reasons why the matter cannot be dealt with over the telephone, such as a set of figures which you have prepared that need careful clarification, or a sample that the client needs to see.

Review topic 9.1

Alfred Tack (1989, p. 85) describes the following as an effective approach, if handled with conviction:

Good morning, Mr Jones, this is Jack Smith of Halliday Publications. I should like to take up just eight minutes of your time to tell you about our new journal for your industry and its wonderful advertising pull. Would Wednesday morning or Wednesday afternoon be more convenient for me to call?

1. What do you think of that general approach?
2. Will Mr Jones react positively or sceptically to 'just eight minutes of your time?'
3. Is offering the choice between two specific times going to increase the chance of a positive response?
4. How would you advise Jack Smith to alter his approach?

It is helpful for the interview request to be connected with a point, such as a letter that the client should have received from you in the previous few days, or a link with someone else – outside or inside the client's organization – who has suggested the contact be made.

(d) Self-presentation and approach

Sales representatives dress in a formal, almost stylized, way in dark suits, with men wearing white shirts and ties and women being likely to wear blouses of more varied colours, although white is most common (Figure 9.2). This indicates that they have taken trouble with their appearance before presenting themselves to the customer, in just the same way as candidates at selection interviews put on their best clothes; but it also masks individuality slightly by being a uniform. Another part of the uniform is the briefcase, which is also the portable office. It seems unwise to depart from these norms.

The uniform then has to be embellished by a purposeful bearing, standing tall and walking briskly, so as to convey that atmosphere of positive confidence suggested earlier. This can go too far and disconcert the client, so it is important to have good bearing without being overbearing.

Although our main focus in this chapter is the sales representative visiting customers at their place of work, there is an interesting summary of effective selling by women counter staff in department stores by Argyle: 'The best salesgirls were very active and talked a lot, but were flexible and could adjust well to different styles of

Figure 9.2 *Sales representatives dress in a formal, almost stylized, way*

interaction. Those who oversold and had goods returned were dominant and made a lot of interruptions' (Argyle, 1972, p. 206).

Encounter

(a) Opening
The exchanges between buyer and seller must be relaxed. Buyers do not readily make decisions if they feel ill at ease or under pressure. This is why the atmosphere of the shopping mall, described earlier, is made as peaceful as possible and the piped music is carefully controlled to be soothing. Opening an interview with a prospective buyer, you must be relaxed yourself as a preliminary to relaxing the buyer.

Methods of relaxation sound strange when described, but can be very effective if run through for a few minutes on a park bench or in the car park before going in for the interview.

● *Muscular relaxation*. Sit comfortably, close your eyes and concentrate, one-by-one, on relaxing the different areas of muscle in your body.

Start with the head and neck – forehead, eyelids, cheeks, chin, neck – focusing on relaxing one at a time before moving on to the next. Gradually move down through your body.

- *Breathing.* Breathe in through your nose to the steady count of three and out through your mouth to a steady count of nine. Do this three times and then breathe in to a steady count of four and out to twelve. After three of those your breathing should be even, but you may want to go to five in and fifteen out.

- *Images.* Conjure up a peaceful image and concentrate on the details for a few minutes: waves gently lapping on a sea shore, deer grazing in early morning woodland or clouds moving across a landscape are useful examples. Going through the lines of a favourite poem might help as you dwell on the different features, conjuring up pictures in your mind's eye. If you have not got a suitable favourite poem, try the opening lines of William Wordsworth, 'On Revisiting the Banks of the Wye';

> Five years have passed; five summers with the length
> Of five long winters; and again I hear
> These waters, rolling from their mountain springs
> With a sweet inland murmur. Once again
> Do I behold these steep and lofty cliffs,
> Which, on a wild secluded scene, impress
> Thoughts of more deep seclusion, and connect
> The landscape with the quiet of the sky.

Relaxation also aids the effective use of the voice. Nervousness and tension make people run out of breath in speaking, as well as making them forget what they intended to say, but your voice in the sales opening has to convey your positive confidence, your responsiveness to the buyer and confirm the first impression given by your dress and bearing, as well as carrying the main sales message.

To make effective use of your voice you must enunciate clearly, so that you can be heard and understood, without sounding artificial or rehearsed. This can be aided by practising with tongue-twisters. Try these:

- A shot-silk sash shop sells shot-silk sashes.
- Six thick thistle sticks.
- Put the cut pumpkin in a pipkin.
- Literally literary.

Another type of exercise is saying phrases that it is easy to mispronounce:

- Laid in the cold ground (not coal ground).
- Would that all difference of sects (not sex) were at an end.
- A sad dangler (not angler).
- She could pain (not pay) nobody.

Clear enunciation, then, needs light and shade. Edward Heath held the office of prime minister, yet invariably spoke in a monotone, making him hard to listen to. In selling you need to vary your tempo, allow the voice to rise and fall, and use emphasis sparingly.

Throughout the opening, the focus of the conversation should be on the buyer, not the seller. Part of the folklore of selling is that the most important thing is 'to sell yourself'. The risk is that representatives do that by being self-centred in their opening remarks and doing most of the talking.'How do you find working here in town? Is the traffic much of a problem?' is more effective than, 'I had the most terrible time getting here this morning, how did you find it?'

Preliminaries, like rapport, are necessary, but should not be prolonged. Five seconds is normally too short a period for two people to get on the same wavelength, but five minutes is too long. The point between those two extremes will be determined by the degree of understanding between the parties that already exists and the nature of the meeting that is to follow. It is, however, the representative that makes the move to proceed.

(b) The presentation
The simplest formula for selling is AIDA:

- Attention
- Interest
- Desire
- Action

Your objective is for the buyer to act – by buying – yet that action will be preceded by going through the three other steps.

Attention will be won by reaching the buyer's motives and needs. The buyer is not interested in the product or service, but will have some motivation related to the product or service that the representative has to reach. This distinction has been well demonstrated by advertising campaigns that have had their impact by selling the following:

- Not the steak, but the sizzle.
- Not the clothes, but their glamour.
- Not the hair spray, but its sex appeal.
- Not the car, but its power.
- Not the timeshare apartment, but holidays in the sun.

Advertising campaigns can only appeal to a narrow range of motives: you can not sell a car's daredevil power and potential for high-speed mountain driving at the same time as selling its potential for carrying small children safely. The sales representative has the opportunity to identify a particular set of motives and needs and sell to them.

Motives may be rational or irrational, they may be held consciously or unconsciously. Here are some examples.

A computerized management-information system could mean one of the following:
- more efficient storage of information and access to it;
- the opportunity to manipulate information to make projections;
- fewer clerical staff;
- being seen to be up-to-date by one's colleagues;
- having a new toy;
- saving money, improving profitability, and so on.

A home-security installation could mean one of the following:
- less fear of intruders and personal danger;
- less fear of losing expensive possessions;
- less fear of losing items of sentimental value;
- increasing the resale value of the house;
- reducing insurance premiums;
- making up for the loss of a dog;
- keeping up with the neighbours, and so on.

The representative needs to identify the client's needs and motives, by knowing about the state of the business, by keeping careful records of previous meetings, by observation of the buyer's situation, by listening for clues and by asking questions.

The presentation of the product or service is then directed specifically at those needs, avoiding the risk of the 'standard spiel', which is the method, for instance, of the market trader, who has no alternative but to present wares in a standard way addressing a set of stereotyped assumptions about the motives and needs of the ten or twenty people who have gathered to see what is going on.

Although the presentation will be varied to suit the particular customer, the representative will have a small stock of standard phrases and sentences, like advertising slogans, that will be suitable in most situations because they describe so succinctly a particular feature of what you are selling:

- 'You pay nothing for the first two years.'
- 'There is no need to prime or seal.'
- 'An average annual increase of x per cent over the last ten years.'

- '94 per cent of service calls answered within the hour: job done within the day.'
- 'Keep upkeep down.'

All buyers have doubts and no order is clinched until those doubts have been resolved, but the representative does not suggest them by saying 'Some people claim that our gearboxes break down after strenuous use, but our tests show . . . ' Doubts or objections have to be handled in two different ways. Real problems have to be made less significant in the customer's mind before he or she voices them; minor problems are best tackled when – and only when – the customer mentions them.

The real problems are not explicitly referred to in the representative's presentation, but the presentation tends to include a number of points that weaken the critical argument. In the gearbox example above, the representative might make gearbox durability a strong feature of the presentation. If it is an insuperable problem – the gearboxes really do break down earlier than they should – then an associated benefit could feature in the presentation, such as free replacement services, or cheap cost of replacements. If there is no compensating feature, you have trouble.

Minor problems are best dealt with when they are raised by the customer first because the customer has to talk about something in order to retain a self-image of someone who is shrewd and not easily persuaded. No buyer will thank you for explaining things so clearly and sign the order there and then. Usually they will be considering alternatives and will express their doubts about your product in terms of the strengths of others. This enables you to address only the problem that is seen by that particular buyer, and you deal with it by allowing full rein to the buyer's doubts, which are then discussed thoroughly. The buyer then has the confidence of having aired the reservations and being convinced by the arguments, playing a positive, or even leading, part in the decision-making. There is no sense of being pre-empted, rushed or convinced against one's better judgement.

(c) Closing

The sale is not made until the order is placed or the buyer's commitment made explicit. Buyers do not like to be rushed, because they feel they are losing control of the situation. Sales representatives are very keen to get the order because they know that 'time to think it over' can frequently mean time for a competitor to present a better price, or for the buyer to decide the item is not wanted anyway.

There are all sorts of promotional devices to expedite decisions, like special offers or discounts, which all have a finishing date. Promotional offers usually last for several weeks, so that there is a small encouragement to the buyer to procrastinate but there is soon a strong incentive to order before the opportunity lapses.

Apart from the support of these devices, every representative eventually has to manipulate the selling encounter to try and obtain the order. The methods of doing this are first to sell step by step, so that throughout the development of the interview the buyer is agreeing with the various points of the presentation, probably being asked to indicate agreement:

- 'That does seem to meet your technical specification precisely, doesn't it?'
- 'This could save you quite you lot of time, couldn't it?'
- 'Don't you think it is a really eye-catching design?'

This progression means that the buying decision is boiled down to one or two final issues rather than the buyer thinking that there are a number of very good features, but it still needs a lot of thinking about.

Representatives should not be reluctant, at the right time, to ask directly for the order. The buyer may often welcome a release from uncertainty by having the question put directly. Also, the representative should look carefully for the time to close, which can sometimes be very soon indeed. Some buyers have decided to buy before you call and do not want to be treated to your carefully prepared presentation: all they want is the answer to two questions and then you out of the way as quickly as possible.

Follow-up

(a) Check completion
Make sure that the order is actually placed and the details are correct; then check that delivery is made and that the buyer is aware that that stage is complete. It may also be necessary to ensure that your company's invoice is settled.

(b) Check satisfaction
By further visits or phone calls check that your product or service is doing its job to the satisfaction of the customer, but do not overdo this solicitude.

(c) Keep records

Keep a record on every person you sell to: a few personal details, so that you can ask about the skiing holiday on the way into the office next time; but also a note of how the client 'plays' the selling interview. In this way you can match your presentation to the buyer's method – quick and to the point or leisurely, light or serious, price-dominant or specification-dominant and so forth.

Table 9.1 *Selling in department stores*

Following research by himself and Mary Lydall, Argyle (1972) suggests the following sequence for sales assistants in department stores (S = sales assistant; C = customer):

1. S makes rapid initial assessment of C to place in a stereotyped category (e.g. 'peppery colonels').

2. S makes first contact with C, either by responding to a question or by drawing C into conversation.

3. S finds out C's needs by responding to C's opening (e.g. 'I would like to buy a tie.') with a series of questions to identify the section of the product range likely to be suitable.

4. S shows a range of goods, starting with a selection guided by the initial assessment in step 1. It may be the most expensive shown first, the middle of the range or the cheapest. Careful study of C's reaction will identify more precisely than stage 3 the appropriate item.

5. S gives information and advice.

6. S clinches the sale on the basis of the developed assessment of C's likely response after the first five stages. Some Cs make up their own minds without prompting, while others need help ('Will you take it now, Madam, or shall we deliver it?').

7. While dealing with payment and delivery, S follows up by giving more information to improve C's feelings of satisfaction, and suggests further related purchases.

Table 9.2 *The selling sequence*

Preparation
1. Decide specific objectives for the interview.
2. Find out and remember:
    - the name of the client;
    - other background information about the client and the company.
3. Obtain the interview by:
    - getting through to the client personally;
    - agreeing a time and date;
    - having good reasons why talking on the telephone is not enough;
    - having a point of reference for the telephone call.
4. Present yourself by:
    - formal dress;
    - purposeful bearing.

Encounter
1. Open by:
    - being relaxed;
    - speaking clearly and not in a monotone;
    - focusing on the client;
    - not prolonging the preliminaries.
2. Present by:
    - identifying the client's needs and motives;
    - addressing those needs and motives and avoiding a standardized presentation;
    - having a stock of words and phrases that are particularly telling;
    - ensuring the client's doubts or reservations are dealt with in conversation.
3. Close by:
    - selling step-by-step;
    - (sometimes) asking for the order;
    - spotting the right time to close.

Follow-up
1. Check completion.
2. Check satisfaction.
3. Keep records.

References

Argyle, M. (1972) *The Psychology of Interpersonal Behaviour*, Penguin Books, Harmondsworth, Middlesex.

Tack, A. (1989) *How to Succeed in Selling*, Cedar Books, London.

Exercise 9a

Strike up a conversation with a stranger at a party, on a train, in a pub or similar public place where your intentions are not likely to be misconstrued (those of you in middle-age should, for instance, avoid approaching seventeen-year-olds in discos – sorry!).

Take particular care to be responsive to the other person, not to interrupt and not to become irritated. Be positive and confident. Afterwards review your performance.

- Did you meet resistance that you were able to overcome?
- Did you pick up the right clues from the other person?
- Did the other person eventually find the conversation pleasant, or at least inoffensive?

Are you the sales type?

Exercise 9b

There is an idea that you have been meaning to put to one of your friends or colleagues for some time, but you have not got round to it so far because you anticipate rejection. Work out an approach based on the ideas in this chapter, prepare carefully and have a go.

If you succeed, discuss with the other person why you were successful. If you fail, repeat exercise 9a!

10 Problem-solving: Counselling

Counselling is a necessary management art which is little understood and rarely practised. People are just as likely to have knotty problems to solve at work as they are in other aspects of their lives. They will be uncertain about whether they are in the job appropriate to their interests and skills, whether they have prospects for change or growth in the job or in the organization that meet their aspirations, and about whether their aspirations are known. They may have problems about job security, whether they can cope with technical change and what may be involved in early retirement or redeployment. We must also accept the fact that most people do not like their jobs very much and may be bored, frustrated or alienated. This frequently leads to the symptoms of job 'dis-ease', such as high turnover, absence, accidents, drug or alcohol dependence and a high level of employee grievances. In his book about counselling, Michael Megranahan (1989) has full chapters on the following situations: stress, redundancy and change, career counselling, career breaks for women, retirement, performance appraisal, relocation, sexual harassment, Youth Training Scheme, debt, substance misuse, violence, discipline, marital and relationship problems, bereavement, suicide, disability or chronic sickness, AIDS, mental health.

There are often difficulties about working relationships within small groups and between superior and subordinate. Problems like these cannot be eliminated by counselling, but the ability of employees to cope with their surroundings can be enhanced by talking through their worry with a competent person; their adjustment becomes better and their contribution improves.

The necessary management art of counselling can improve the fit between employee expectation of the organization and organizational expectation of the employee. It is, however, an art little practised in Britain, although more widespread in the United States.

A definition of counselling by Pietrofesa *et al.* (1978) helps us to both understand the activity and see some of the differences between British and American practice:

> Counselling is a relationship between a professionally trained, competent counsellor and an individual seeking help in gaining greater self-understanding and improved decision-making and behavior-change skills for problem resolution and/or developmental growth . . . . It is not giving tests, providing information, giving advice or gathering data in an interview. (Pietrofesa *et al.*, 1978, p. 6)

Counselling is gradually being professionalized, but there are still few professionally trained counsellors in the field of employment and even fewer in the ranks of management. Furthermore, it is still less common in the United Kingdom than in the United States for people to seek this type of assistance. Counselling is typically provided spontaneously and informally without it even being acknowledged as counselling by the person seeking assistance, who will describe it as seeking information – perhaps advice – rather than seeking help in self-understanding. This general self-consciousness and diffidence means that counselling is generally disguised as something else. It may be a continuous feature of the working relationship between two people, it is more likely to come in an interview of some sort, either the semi-formal encounter of performance appraisal or the informal chat stimulated by an incident in day-to-day operations – 'I think we'd better have a talk and try to sort this out.'

Review topic 10.1

In your own managerial role, in what circumstances would you regard it as appropriate to counsel someone employed in the same organization who approached you with one of the following:

1. a marital problem;
2. fears of personal redundancy;
3. work-induced stress;
4. complaints of sexual harassment?

In what ways do you feel your managerial role would constrain, or disqualify, you from offering counselling in these circumstances?

The counsellor as a person

The extensive literature on counselling and its related research show that there is a 'scientific' basis to counselling in that generally effective approaches can be distinguished from generally ineffective approaches; but the personal qualities and flair of the person who is counselling will be a greater determinant of success than any detailed understanding of the research.

> It is not difficult to teach someone who reflects positive counsellor attributes some basic counselling skills and produce an effective counsellor. On the other hand it is unlikely that one can teach helping skills beyond the most superficial to someone who is basically a non-helper. (Pietrofesa *et al.*, 1978, p. 37)

The most thorough analysis of the qualities that make an effective counsellor is by Combs *et al.* (1971) and includes the suggestion that counsellors need to be more concerned with other people than with things and events; that they are concerned about others and not merely with themselves and that they see their role as being to encourage the process of search and discovery rather than working towards a predetermined solution to a particular problem. Above all, counselling is an intimate, open activity, and another reason why it is so rarely practised by managers is the fear of intimacy and of losing status or control in a situation through reducing the social distance between a manager and a subordinate. Also, many managers shy away from counselling because they feel they will not be successful. One quality that the counsellor has to demonstrate to the client is respect, accepting and not disapproving of the client, trusting and being genuinely concerned for the client's welfare. This will be a part of the counsellor's philosophy, but it still has to be demonstrated.

Related to, but different from, respect is warmth, creating a feeling of safety and security for the client in the relationship with the counsellor. It cannot be the easy intimacy of relationship with a close friend, but neither can it be contrived: 'avoid effusive and chatty, buddy-buddy behaviour. The salesman's smile, handshake, and strained attempts to be friendly are the antithesis of warmth. Instead the helper should immediately focus on the needs of the helpee and begin to "earn the right to care"' (Gazda, 1973, p. 57).

Authenticity is an aspect of counselling that has received much attention by the professionals, and Carl Rogers came near to believing that it was the only quality that mattered in the counselling relationship. Counsellors must be genuine not only in what they say and the attitudes they display, but also in the extent to which they disclose themselves to the client. This presents problems to people in management positions, who sometimes feel that they have to dissemble or prevaricate in discussion with subordinates because of operational constraints on their freedom to disclose information or their uncertainty about the reliability of information ('It looks as if this person will be moved out of the Marketing Department because of his poor performance, but it is not settled yet. I can't tell him he will be shifted; I can't tell him he won't; better not to say anything').

Empathy is a prerequisite of being able to help with the problems of others in any more than the most superficial way. It has been defined by Rogers (1951) as the ability of the counsellor

> to assume, as far as he is able, the internal frame of reference of the client, to perceive the world as the client sees it, to perceive the client himself as he is seen by himself, to lay aside all perceptions from the external frame of reference while doing so and to communicate something of this empathic understanding to the client. (Rogers, 1951, p. 29)

This is not quite the same as sympathy, where one is sharing the feelings of the other and identifying with those feelings. This is not likely in the relationship between managed and manager, but empathic behaviour is easier.

The approach to counselling

The procedure varies slightly according to the theory one holds about counselling.

The most widely accepted mode is the client-centred approach, pioneered by Rogers in 1942. It is based on the proposition that all human beings have a need for positive regard and this can only be satisfied by others, so that the concept of self we all have is something we develop as a result of what we receive from others. If we then feel a need that conflicts with what we have learned from others, we are likely to categorize it as bad. Client-centred therapy is a way of enabling people to incorporate new experiences with what has been learned previously in order to acquire a more flexible concept of self. In this way there is a move towards self-actualization, the prime motivational force in the individual. The counselling process is one of empathic understanding, in which the counsellor becomes immersed in the world of the client, learning about it and enabling the client to understand it better by the process of sharing experience and making explicit aspects of the world that were previously implicit and not truly known.

The specious appeal to managers of this counselling approach is that it is feasible for the lay person to adopt and comes close to normal everyday behaviour. Rogers made the comment: 'the therapeutic relationship is only a special instance of interpersonal relationships in general, and that the same lawfulness governs all such relationships' (Rogers, 1961, p. 37). Other theoretical approaches are less available to laymen either because of their dependence on high degrees of skill or because of their basis in a professional, doctor–patient type of relationship.

The counselling sequence

Preparation

(a) Counsellor briefing

Counsellors will have trouble if they start absolutely cold with a client, devoid of any information apart from knowing there is a problem. Clergymen and some social workers occasionally have to start in this way, but at least their position as counsellor is clear at the outset. In organizational life it is unlikely that anyone will be so clearly labelled, and the counsellor needs to have some prior briefing about the client. There may be some documents such as application forms or performance appraisals; there may be a background of knowing the prospective client through everyday working contacts or reports from colleagues. The counsellor needs to be able to assimilate this material without reaching conclusions and deciding the outcome. If experience shows that prior briefing makes it difficult for an individual counsellor to avoid preconceptions it may be better to begin with only the sketchiest of information in order to avoid distortion.

(b) Nature of the interview

How often do counselling encounters take place with both counsellor and client sharing the same perception of what the encounter is for? It must be the minority of lay counselling interviews that start like that. More often they will develop either spontaneously for both parties or at the initiative of one that was not expected by the other. The difficulty lies in the lack of acknowledgement in organizations of the value of counselling and its place in working relationships. Management development officers are not expected to initiate counselling interviews with trainees, they are expected to tell them how they are getting on. Employees do not expect counselling from their superiors; they may ask for information or advice.

In some circumstances a discussion between two people at work develops into a counselling event, but more often they are as the result of an intention by one person that has then to be shared with, understood and accepted by, the other.

An example was the case of Nick, a management trainee who was feeling disenchanted with the training scheme he had joined a few months earlier. He had only the vaguest ideas about what to do, so he went 'to have a word with' the training officer, Helen Pritchard, intending to resign, or to complain, to ask for a change or possibly to ask for a review of his progress. When he arrived at Helen Pritchard's office the question he actually put was about car parking! It was such a bizarre question, and Nick's demeanour was so peculiar that she had to decide what the question meant. There was no clear request for counselling, but Helen Pritchard decided there was a latent content to the inquiry other than the manifest content, as was described by Roethlisberger and Dickson (1939, pp. 225-59) in their early studies. They found frequent situations where a deep-rooted problem was signalled in an oblique way.

Some managers go to extremes in injecting awesome significance into the most innocent comment, like the supervisor who would not accept that the request by a woman no longer to work overtime at the weekend meant just that, and was not a cry for help because her children had left home, her mother had died or her husband was beating her.

Another example is where a manager may be bothered about the performance of an employee who seems to be lacking enthusiasm, turning in late for work, taking days off or whatever the symptom may be. If the manager decides to 'have a word with' the employee, the hierarchical relationship between the two will make the lack-lustre employee believe that the matter is being raised as a preliminary to some form of punishment, inhibiting the likelihood of employee openness. To avoid the risk of client apprehension or defensiveness being too great, managers in that situation are likely to conceal what they want to talk about until the conversation itself begins.

Situations like these require the nature of the ensuing conversation to be shared and accepted by both participants before it can begin.

Review topic 10.2

In the situation described at the end of section (b), how would you deal with a request from the employee that a union representative should be present during the conversation? In what ways do you think this would be helpful? In what ways would it jeopardize the prospects of a fruitful discussion?

(c) Counsellor authority

The counsellor needs to be someone who can speak with authority. All the emphasis in the preceding few pages has been on counselling as a process whereby people improve their personal adjustment to their situation, so that the counsellor needs all those qualities of empathy, respect, warmth and authenticity which have been mentioned. When counselling takes place within the employment relationship there is the additional element that the counsellor needs to be in a position to take some action about that employment relationship. A typical outcome of this sort of counselling is some change in perception and behaviour by the employee, accompanied by some changes, initiated by the counsellor, in the work situation to reinforce the changes the client is making.

Being moved onto a different shift, given extra training, being reassigned to less hazardous work or some similar action are examples of how action by the client in enabled and complemented.

The counsellor therefore needs to be in a position to bring about that sort of change. The client has to be worth talking to both in the sense of being able to make things happen to the context and enabling changes to take place in the content of the job.

Another aspect of counsellor authority is the perceived competence in making judgements about the job. However non-evaluative the counselling approach, it is not so bland as to eliminate any evaluation at all. To some extent the straight opinion of the counsellor will be sought and will be needed. This requires understanding of the job the client is doing, other jobs in the organization and the overall economic position of the business.

(d) Location and setting

The counselling interaction tends to take a long time. This is another reason why it is often avoided by managers. If it were professional counselling it might be protracted over several meetings, but that would introduce an element of formality inappropriate in organizational life, where there is seldom more than one session and a follow-up meeting to check on progress. For this reason the location needs to be one in which two people can have a private, uninterrupted conversation for an hour or more without arousing speculation about what they are up to. The nature of the encounter is going to be more informal than most of those discussed in this book and the setting should therefore help this informality:

> eye-ball to eye-ball confrontation over yards of mahogany desk may help bolster your authority in a tough disciplinary interview, but for most purposes the interviewee will talk more freely if he is comfortably seated and can see the interviewer clearly without being obliged to stare straight at him. (Hackett, 1981, p. 17)

Encounter

(a) Rapport

The special nature of rapport in the counselling interview is that it determines whether or not the interview itself will take place. In selection, training or discipline, rapport is needed to ensure a useful interview. In counselling it is needed to set up sufficient trust and understanding for anything to be done at all. Without it being done satisfactorily, the client may not disclose any real concerns and may not be committed to a frank exchange:

> Errors in understanding the client may result in his hasty withdrawal. And usually it is in this interview that the client decides whether the counselling relationship is the method he will use in his attempts to work out his difficulties. (Porter, 1973, p. 88)

Establishing rapport therefore takes longer than with other inter- actions. The counsellor will show respect and warmth and will demonstrate attentive listening to the client, as the client (rather than the counsellor or the 'problem') becomes the focus of the conver- sation. This is difficult because few of us can forget ourselves to that extent. Also, the confused, emotionally charged outburst that is either unleashed or being suppressed is not easy to attend to.

Counsellors need to guard against listening that is too keen, inserting too many questions to clarify, check facts and so forth. The need for clarity has to be subordinated – at the beginning – to the need for mutual respect and candour.

Throughout the interview, but especially in rapport, the counsellor will model behaviour for the client. The counsellor's equanimity will help to calm the client, the counsellor's confidence will reduce the client's uncertainty and attentive listening may help the client become attentive as the interaction proceeds.

(b) Factual interchange

As the rapport develops the counsellor can move into a more direct discussion of the issue lying at the heart of the meeting. This takes the form of the counsellor developing a discussion that is a non-controversial exchange of factual information, a review of what they both know about the situation and a sharing of what one knows but the other does not. The counsellor is deliberately deferring analysis and opinion; not inviting the client to express feelings but putting together a data base for them both to use later.

This is similar to the doctor collecting evidence when visiting a patient. Putting questions about the location of the pain, how long it has been there, and whether there has been any dizziness, sickness or diarrhoea, is putting together the information that is needed for the diagnosis. It is also getting the patient to reflect on the situation in a practical way. Furthermore, the doctor is providing some reassurance by giving off an impression of reassuring expertise and by providing fragments of information. When you are feeling like death, it is initially irritating but soon reassuring to be told, 'There's a lot of this about' or 'You're the fourth person I've seen this morning with the same problem.' You still feel awful, but you begin to believe that you will survive.

The counsellor is collecting basic information on the situation about which the client will later be expressing hopes or fears, showing to the client some knowledge, and opening up the exchanges between them on a low key.

(c) Opinion interchange

The second interchange is when the counsellor and client exchange opinions about the facts. Usually the counsellor will move to this phase by inviting comment from the client, 'Well, how do you feel about things generally?' or 'But you still feel that you are getting a raw deal?' or some similar opener.

It is important at this stage to avoid criticism of the client or decision-making about what is to be done regarding the issue being discussed. This can be difficult, as the client will usually start with a feeling of guilt or apprehension and will either be anticipating criticism or will interpret innocent remarks as being critical. The objective, however, is for the matter to be opened up and understood by both parties. The counsellor is hearing the client's views, anxieties, apprehensions and hopes, to build a fuller mental picture of what they are discussing, adding the opinions to the basic facts. The client is also coming to understand the matter better through articulating feelings. Feelings have to be expressed, and thoughts have to be marshalled before they can be expressed. The unburdening helps to make the true nature of the problem clearer.

The counsellor will mainly use the technique of reflection at this stage rather than too many questions, so that the client is helped to examine what is being said and comprehend it more fully (Figure 10.1).

Figure 10.1 *Reflection will help the client to examine what is said and comprehend it more fully*

The counsellor's direct input is to provide reassurance or encouragement, particularly if the client is being self-critical and showing a shortage of self-confidence. The counsellor may point out aspects of the client's job performance that are more positive and satisfactory than the shortcomings on which the client is tending to dwell. While avoiding the trap of patronizing the client, it may be useful to invoke positive comments that have been made by other powerful members of the organization about the job performance. It may be possible to say that no decisions have yet been made about early retirement or factory closure. Whatever the topic being discussed, there will be some encouraging comments that the counsellor can make. This does not lull the client into a false sense of security; it helps to establish a realistic sense of security, after which some searching joint problem-solving can be attempted.

In the job performance and working situation of every one of us there are some good aspects and some that are not so good. Counselling can help to strengthen the good and modify the not-so-good, and clients will be more able to examine their situation constructively if the examination follows some reassurance and confirmation of their self-esteem:

> With all troublesome situations the counsellor provides a sense of hopefulness. This does not mean inappropriate or false reassurances. Hopefulness is a positive attitude that suggests there are solutions to most problems and that the manager is willing to invest some time in helping his subordinate find them. (Mayerson, 1979, p. 288)

(d) Joint problem-solving

There is now a shift of emphasis from encouragement by the counsellor to analysis by the client, who is invited by the counsellor to expand on the major features of the problem that have been opened up. Clients move away from 'getting it off their chest' towards analysing their feelings and their situation, looking for causes and explanations. The initiative in analysis comes from the client, although the counsellor provides listening and understanding, with occasional questions and reflection to sharpen the focus and make connections.

It is very tempting at this stage for the counsellor to get carried away by a desire to be helpful – and to get the interview over – by offering solutions. This is a particular problem for a manager, whose style of behaviour may be geared to making decisions for and about subordinates, and the client may be looking for this approach. The assumption underlying client analysis is that what clients say and understand they have begun to acknowledge and may be able to cope with, so that actions rooted in this analysis have a chance of working. On the other hand, analysis produced by another – even a respected and respectful counsellor – may in some way or other be screened out by the client through cognitive dissonance. This is why the emphasis is on the client's own analysis. Part of the counsellor's contribution may, however, be to confront the client with any inconsistencies in that analysis.

It is in this stage of the interaction that the counselling succeeds or fails. Either clients break through to a fresh awareness of themselves, their situation and what can be improved, or they remain unaffected and the remainder of the interview is an anti-climax with a further meeting being the only possibility of progress.

(e) Decision-making

Now counsellor and client work out tentative courses of action as a result of the analysis, with both of them having responsibility for implementation. They exchange opinions on solutions to the problem they have examined and gradually commit themselves to action. Some of the action will be taken by the counsellor, who can remove some impediments within the organization or open up opportunities; some action will be taken by the client altering behaviour in line with the changes to the working context that the counsellor is making.

The counsellor helps at this point to generate alternatives for the client to consider, arising either out of different experience and a different viewpoint or by interpretation of the client's analysis. Another counsellor contribution is to agree targets with the client for getting things done, as a reinforcer for the agreed actions.

(f) Disengagement

Disengaging from this encounter involves attention to the future, so that any benefits from the exchanges are not lost. Apart from target-setting, the counsellor can review in detail what has been discussed to get the client's consent that they share the same understanding. Usually, they will arrange a further meeting to check on progress.

Follow-up

(a) Case notes

If the counsellor makes some notes about the encounter there is a starting point for any other interaction that may follow and a reminder of the action that has been agreed. In some situations these notes can then be shared with the client so that an agreed version is produced. This has the advantage of confirming with the client what is going to happen and making the action less imprecise. The disadvantage is the extent to which the client will feel tied down by such a statement and find it inconsistent with the intimate, informal conversations that took place during the interview. With many clients the appropriate action would be made less likely if it were written up in a 'contract' with the counsellor.

(b) Counsellor action

Client action will always be to change some aspect of personal behaviour. Counsellor action can be more varied, depending not only upon the nature of the problem but also upon its deep-rootedness. The easy counselling interviews are those where the problem is resolved by the exchanges of the interaction itself: a misunderstanding is cleared up or a piece of crucial information is provided. The counsellor will need to do little more in follow-up than produce confirmation. Where difficulties are more entrenched and require great effort by the client, the action by the counsellor will need to be more significant if it is to enable the client to be successful. Among the more effective counsellor actions might be changing the job the client is doing or its location, as the job itself or the superior–subordinate relationship are the most common causes of problems at work.

Table 10.1 *The counselling sequence*

Preparation
1. Review:
   - any relevant documents.
2. Check:
   - any background information;
   - the nature of the interview;
   - the authority of the counsellor;
   - the appropriateness of the setting: time, privacy and relative informality.

Encounter
1. Start with:
   - rapport.
2. Develop through three sets of interchanges:
   - factual;
   - opinion;
   - joint problem-solving.
3. Conclude with:
   - decision-making;
   - disengagement.

Follow-up
1. Complete:
   - case notes.
2. Take:
   - counsellor action.

References

Beveridge, W.E. (1968) *Problem-solving Interviews*, Allen & Unwin, London.
Combs, A., D. Avila and W. Purkey, (1971) *Helping Relationships*, Allyn & Bacon, Boston.
Gazda, G. (1973) *Human Relations Development*, Allyn & Bacon, Boston.
Hackett, P. (1981) *Interview Skills Training*, 2nd edn., Institute of Personnel Management, London.
Mayerson, E. N. (1979) *Shoptalk*, Saunders, Philadelphia.
Megranahan, M. (1989) *Counselling: A practical guide for employers*, Institute of Personnel Management, London.
Pietrofesa, J. J., A. Hoffman, H. H. Splete, and D. V. Pinto, (1978) *Counselling: Theory, research and practice*, Rand McNally, Chicago.
Porter, E. H. (1973) *Introduction to Therapeutic Counselling*, Houghton Mifflin, Boston, MA.
Roethlisberger, F. J. and W. J. Dickson, (1939) *Management and the Worker*, Harvard University Press.
Rogers, C. R. (1951) *Client-centred Therapy*, Houghton Mifflin, Boston, MA.
Rogers, C. R. (1961) *On Becoming a Person*, Houghton Mifflin, Boston, MA.

Exercise 10a

A specialized technique, referred to in Chapter 3 is reflection, which is reflecting back a respondent's comment to get more comment on the same topic. It is especially appropriate for counselling and was neatly defined by Beveridge:

> a selective form of listening in which the listener picks out the emotional overtones of a statement and 'reflects' these back to the respondent without any attempt to evaluate them . . . the interviewer expresses neither approval or disapproval, neither sympathy or condemnation. (1968, p. 57)

In the next few conversations you have, practise reflection and see what effect it has on the development of the exchanges with the other person.

Exercise 10b

This exercise needs the co-operation of your spouse, other trusted relative or close friend.

1. Identify an incident that the other person experienced some time in the past, which was unpleasant or disconcerting at the time, but the wounds of which have now healed.

2. Take the respondent through the events again, using the sequence suggested in this chapter, including decision-making to agree on what should have been done.

3. Change roles and repeat the process with an incident from your past.

11 Problem-solving: Discipline

Many contemporary views of discipline are connected with the idea of punishment; a disciplinarian is one seen as an enforcer of rules, a hard taskmaster or martinet. To discipline school children is usually to punish them by keeping them in after school or chastising them. Disciplinary procedures in employment are usually drawn up to provide a preliminary to dismissal to ensure that the eventual dismissal will not be viewed as unfair by a tribunal. The late 1980s has seen an increasing management attention to absence control. Paul Edwards reports:

> There appears to be growing managerial concern about absenteeism and timekeeping . . . . There has been a move towards closer monitoring of attendance and the enforcement of standards. In one firm subjected to case study analysis, absence control was high on the managerial agenda . . . workers were more aware of pressures to work harder and tightening discipline. (Edwards, 1989, p. 320)

This situation makes a problem-solving approach to discipline difficult for a manager, as there is always the overall impression of them-and-us control in the background making it unlikely that the employee will see the manager's behaviour as being authentic in the way that was seen as necessary in the last chapter.

Despite the difficulties, this chapter is based on the more accurate notion of discipline implied in its derivation from the Latin *discere*, 'to learn' and *discipulus* 'learner'. In disciplinary interviews the manager is attempting to modify the working behaviour of a subordinate, but it does not necessarily involve punishment. The aim of the interview is to achieve an adjustment of some aspect of employee behaviour to make it consistent with the objectives of the organization. It is reasonable to argue that self-discipline is the most effective, as well as the most dignified, method of ensuring this consistency, and often it is the only means available. When there is self-discipline there is little need for supervisory controls and unless supervisory controls are withdrawn, self-discipline is not likely to develop.

There are three elements in a system of discipline. First, there are rules and arrangements broadly acceptable to both employer and employee. These provide a framework of organizational justice to ensure general compliance with the rules because they are seen as worthy of support. This is a limitation on the freedom of action of managers, as it requires them to behave in a controlled and consistent manner. There will be many rules and arrangements, some formal and written down, some informal and understood. The formal are likely to include such features as rules about not smoking, punctuality and safety. The informal understandings will be mainly about conventions of behaviour and relationships.

The second element of the system is managerial control of individual and small-group performance to ensure compliance with the rules and to correct deviations. The correct guarding of machinery by employees will normally be supervised, at least while a person is learning the job in the early stages of a person's employment. The observance of times at which people start and finish work will be monitored, not only to obtain the employer's pound of flesh, but also to avoid dissatisfaction among employees about those who appear not to be abiding by the rules that everyone else is following. This control is only operated in relation to individual employees:

> whereas so-called group 'indiscipline' normally results from a widespread rejection of a working arrangement or rule and the resolution of any conflict lies in the negotiation of new work standards, individual indiscipline indicates merely a personal deviation from standards generally accepted by other employees. (Department of Employment, (1973, p. 2)

Managerial control of individual performance can only be exercised satisfactorily if there is a framework of rules, and the third element of the discipline system is only possible in the presence of managerial control. This latter element is what the other two are used to produce: self-discipline, or individual control of own performance to meet organizational objectives within a framework of organizational justice. It may seem that managerial control and individual control are not consistent: how can there be one with the other? The answer is that managerial control is needed to provide the learning that is a prerequisite of the self-discipline. The skilled craftsman acquires the autonomy and independence of his skilled status as a result of close supervision during an apprenticeship, and the sales representative acquires the freedom of the road after close schooling in the features of the product and the market in which it is necessary to operate.

Even when someone is technically accomplished there may still be a need for managerial control. This is not the place to discuss the various theories of leadership, but the most accomplished performers in entertainment and the arts often lean heavily on a producer or conductor to enable them to produce the performance. In sport there are instances of a gifted player performing brilliantly under one captain and moderately under another. There is, therefore, some balance to be struck between managerial control and individual control. The manager, or monitor of performance, has to judge when to reduce supervision and by how much.

In any occupation there is a proper area for external control – like quality sampling or the annual audit of the books – but there is also the area for self-control that cannot be invaded by the superior without jeopardizing performance and impairing the manager–subordinate relationship.

Dealing with individual incidents of indiscipline will always be affected by the adequacy of the three components of a discipline system that have been described, and all of which are needed. The manager attempting to deal with a disciplinary matter in an organization that lacks a satisfactory framework of justice will have a very hard task. That framework has to fit within the legal framework, and no approach to discipline is complete without an understanding of the current legislative position on dismissal and employment rights, although these are not included in this chapter.

Review topic 11.1

Think of three examples from your own experience of the three different types of discipline:

1. Organizational justice
   (a) _____
   (b) _____
   (c) _____
2. Managerial control
   (a) _____
   (b) _____
   (c) _____
3. Self-discipline
   (a) _____
   (b) _____
   (c) _____

More extensive consideration of discipline in employment can be found in Torrington and Hall (1987, pp. 455–72), Salamon (1987, pp. 503–34) and the seminal article by Huberman (1964). This chapter is based on the assumption that the disciplinary interview is one in which the manager is dealing with a situation in which there is a need for managerial control of individual performance, but not necessarily requiring a dressing down or rebuke. This may be needed, but until the manager has determined what is causing the unsatisfactory performance we cannot know whether that is appropriate or inappropriate.

The discipline sequence

Preparation

(a) Procedural position

With the unfortunate overtones of sanction that bedevil any disciplinary interview, the manager needs first to check the procedural position. In some cases the likelihood of penalties will already have been set up by earlier interviews at which formal warnings may have been given. In that case the scope for problem-solving is limited, as the procedural machinery has begun to grind inexorably, making further warnings or penalties difficult to avoid. Most interviews, however, precede procedure and the parties are less inhibited by procedural considerations. The manager needs to emphasize the informality of the encounter, keeping procedural implications at bay.

In procedure there is the likelihood of the employee being represented; out of procedure representation is less likely, although the employee may feel anxious and threatened without it.

(b) Evidence

Disciplinary interviews always start at the behest of the management (when people start asking to be disciplined, you really will have problems) so the manager will need to collect evidence together before beginning the encounter. This will include some basic details about the respondent, but mainly it will be information about the aspects of the working performance that are unsatisfactory and why. Too often this exists only in opinions that have been offered and prejudices that are held. This provides a poor basis for a constructive interview, so you need to ferret out details, with as much factual corroboration as possible, including a shrewd guess about the respondent's view.

It is almost inevitable that the respondent will start the interview defensively, expecting to be blamed for something and therefore ready to refute any allegations, probably deflecting blame elsewhere. The manager needs to anticipate the respondent's initial reaction and be prepared to deal with the reaction as well as with facts that have been collected. Unless the impending encounter is at an early, informal stage, the manager also needs to know about earlier warnings, cautions or penalties that have been invoked.

(c) Participants

Who will be present when the encounter takes place? The most obvious person is the one whose contribution to organizational objectives is being doubted – the possibly 'guilty' party. The more difficult question is whether or not the respondent will be accompanied by a representative. The manager will usually feel it better to avoid such representation at an early, informal stage on the grounds that the presence of a representative makes the proceedings more formal and 'denies the flexibility of discussion and problem-solving that a one-to-one encounter can offer. The respondent, on the other hand, may feel so vulnerable if confronted behind closed doors that representation would be requested as soon as there was a whiff of discipline in the air. In those circumstances the presence of a 'friend' or representative may provide the degree of confidence that is needed to look at the situation in a problem-solving rather than defensive way.

Once an interview takes place in procedure, the manager will be more willing for the employee to be represented, especially if it is a procedural requirement.

What is the role of witnesses? Many disciplinary interviews involve the manager dealing with a matter reported by others and perhaps depending upon verbal evidence. The foreman says the respondent hit him and Frank saw him do it. Do Frank and the foreman come to the interview in case the respondent claims that the foreman started it and Frank wasn't looking anyway?

If the interview is well into the formal stages of procedure, it may be necessary for the witnesses to be produced with all the problems of charge and counter-charge and the difficulty of determining whether the respondent is more sinned against than sinning. Before that stage is reached the manager will do better to handle the matter alone, but will also need to work on the basis of more tangible evidence.

(d) Location

The appropriate location will also vary according to the formality of the proceedings. The early, informal discussion designed to solve a problem before it deteriorates into opposed attitudes and rigid procedure needs an environment similar to that of counselling, to provide the opportunity of empathy and demonstrated respect. The further the situation moves towards sanctions and the possibility of dismissal, the more appropriate a stiff, formal atmosphere becomes. It is not authentic behaviour to invite an employee into your office, provide a cup of coffee and a cigarette and then say in a warm and friendly tone of voice with accompanying smile and eye contact: 'By the way, I think I ought to tell you that you are being dismissed on Friday. I'm really most terribly sorry.'

That sounds ludicrous but is only a slight exaggeration of what can happen as managers try hard to be liked in spite of the bad news they are delivering. No amount of 'niceness' in the way news is conveyed will make more acceptable what is being said, and the wrapping up in honeyed words may make the stark truth hard to understand.

Review topic 11.2

What situations have you experienced, or heard about, where the location of a disciplinary interview was clearly inappropriate?

Unusual formality is appropriate for the later, judicial phases of disciplinary procedure and the large, impressive offices of senior managers make good Star Chambers.

Encounter

(a) Explaining the management position

The encounter is taking place because of management dissatisfaction with the employee's performance. The employee is probably also dissatisfied, and this will become clear in a good encounter, but the starting point is a statement, by the manager, of the management dissatisfaction.

The statement is of facts about an operational problem; it is not a statement of disapproval or moral outrage about the facts, as the manager is dealing with a problem and not – yet, at least – dealing with an indolent or disobedient employee. Whether there is blame to be attached to the employee has yet to be determined. If, for instance, a man is being interviewed about unpunctuality it is inappropriate for the manager to begin by telling him that his behaviour is reprehensible – 'Your timekeeping this week has been disgraceful' – as it might be that the man had a seriously ill child needing constant attendance through the night, and this would make the manager's behaviour reprehensible.

A more even-handed opening statement – 'Each day this week you have been at least twenty minutes late' – is a more effective opening, as it concentrates on the problem without allocating blame. It is also a reasonably precise statement of the facts that is not likely to lead to an argument about values, and it sets a limit on the dissatisfaction, as it specifies only one issue, implying that there is no other problem. If there are other problems, they should also be mentioned.

This comment about the opening needs emphasis first because managers are normally reluctant to handle disciplinary matters firmly. There may be a small minority of people in management posts who enjoy brutalizing their subordinates, but they are probably as far beyond redemption as Captain Bligh and will certainly not be reading this book. Most people dislike having to take up disciplinary questions and tend to broach matters ineffectually, fearful that they will be confounded by the respondent or that the situation will get out of control.

Secondly, there is a tendency for managers to initiate disciplinary measures because an employee simply 'does not come up to scratch'. There is nothing specific, just not a feeling that he is not quite good enough. 'Can't we get rid of him?' Unless there are reasons that one can make explicit and about which something can be done, the disciplinary process has little prospect of success: it is merely a ritual preceding dismissal.

(b) Understanding the employee position

There are two sides to every story, and the manager now asks the employee to say what the reasons are for the problem and for a view of how serious it is. The employee is not, therefore, being asked to give an explanation but to comment on the problem. It is unlikely that all employees will make that nice distinction in their minds, but some will and most will respond to the difference in emphasis.

The manager now gets a different dimension on the problem, as it is looked at from the employee's standpoint. In most cases the reaction is a straightforward account, with the employee explaining why the difficulty has arisen, and the manager can move on to the next stage of the encounter.

The nature of the employee reaction can be problematic. Some, for instance, may not understand when there is a management problem.

- 'Why should twenty minutes lateness in the morning matter when I stay an extra half an hour in the evening?'

- 'Why so much fuss about using colourful language in conversation with the supervisor? In my last job everyone did it.'

Another problem can be when the employee is not willing to talk about the matter at all, through being apprehensive or as a result of not wanting to discuss personal matters, or perhaps because of not wanting to implicate anyone else. A third difficulty can be angry defiance from the respondent, who feels an injustice in the situation that is developing.

(c) Examining the problem

After these first two stages in the encounter, the manager will have reached the point where the respondent knows that there is management dissatisfaction about a specified aspect of what has happened, and will have explained a different point of view on the problem described. Now is the time to move towards a solution, with action by the manager, by the employee or by both. As in counselling, it is not realistic to view the encounter as one that ends with all the follow-up action being taken by the respondent, who proceeds in the future to behave instead of misbehaving. It is just as likely that some management action is needed to remove an impediment.

If a local van driver is developing the habit of being drunk during the late afternoon, one solution is for him to stop drinking during the day, another might be to dismiss him forthwith, but a third might be to change his duties to fork-truck driving inside the factory where it is less likely for him to be able to drink on duty. If a computer officer is constantly arguing with a supervisor and questioning orders she receives, one solution would be for her to stop being disobedient, but another might be to shift her to another job where the relationship with a different supervisor would be less abrasive and would enable her to develop compliant behaviour.

A familiar argument against this type of reasoning is that managers should not have to pander to employees in this way. Going to work involves some inconvenience and places obligations on employees that have to be met, and employees not able or willing to meet these obligations should make way for someone who can and will.

That is a statement of a particular, macho point of view about how people ought to behave. If, however, there is a problem about the working behaviour of an employee that can easily be overcome by a small administrative change, it seems worth doing, especially if it is a problem that the employee cannot otherwise resolve. Managers who want to adopt a take-it-or-leave-it approach are unlikely to win the level of support and commitment that is needed to run an effective operation. Furthermore, if managers are going to take the time and trouble to conduct problem-solving interviews on disciplinary issues it is realistic for them to go one step further and see if there is some practical step that can be taken either to enable the employee performance to alter, or to reinforce some resolution on a change that the employee may make as a result of the encounter.

It is also necessary to point out that not all respondents in disciplinary situations follow a 'reasonable' management lead. Some are looking for a fight (Figure 11.1), some are looking for a point of principle on which to make a stand, some will always throw a tantrum or burst into tears and some are attention seekers.

Figure 11.1 *Some respondents act aggressively in disciplinary situations*

The process of clarifying the problem and 'holding it up to the light', as it were, so that both manager and respondent can see it and look at it from different angles, may be enough to produce the solution. Both parties agree on what is to be done and agree to do it, so that the encounter can move to a conclusion.

(d) Dealing with the unresponsive respondent

Clarifying the problem may be enough to produce a solution to it, but if the employee will not respond, there is now a test of the power behind the manager's authority. There are at least three further steps that can be taken one after the other until one of them is effective. In some situations the manager will move straight to the final step, omitting steps one and two.

1. *Persuasion*. The first step is to point out that there are aspects of what the respondent may want to achieve that will not come about unless there is a change in behaviour:

- 'If your output doesn't meet the standard by the end of the training period, your earnings will drop.'

- 'Good timekeeping is an absolute must for anyone wanting a transfer into Inspection.'

There is a powerful inducement to respondents when they see that it is in their own interests to alter what they have been doing.

2. *Disapproval*. Some people are more concerned to be well regarded by others than to pursue their own best interests, so they may respond to a suggestion that their behaviour is displeasing those whose goodwill they wish to keep:

- 'The Management Development Panel are rather disappointed.'

- 'Other people in the department feel you are not pulling your weight.'

Alternatively, the manager taking the interview may take a personal lead:

- This simply is not good enough in a competitive industry like ours.'

- 'If this happens again, it will certainly be a formal warning, and the next step would be dismissal.'

3. *Penalties*. If all else fails, or if the other possible moves to disengagement prove to be inappropriate, penalties have to be used. This will be either with an obdurate employee or when there is a serious offence about which there is no doubt. The most common penalty is the formal warning that comes as a preliminary to possible dismissal, but other possibilities are relocation or demotion, which move the respondent to a job that is less attractive. Suspension with or without pay removes the employee from the workplace for a short period without terminating the contract (Figure 11.2). All of these are penalties that fall short of dismissal. In situations that are sufficiently grave, summary dismissal is both appropriate and feasible within the legal framework.

Figure 11.2 *Suspension with pay*

(e) Disengagement

The move to disengagement may come at any one of the four points mentioned above. How does the manager handle the close of the encounter? In some ways the easiest situation is summary dismissal, as the employment relationship is going to end and the only considerations are of the procedural fairness and administrative accuracy with which it is done, so as to reduce the possibility of a tribunal hearing.

If the outcome of the encounter is anything other than dismissal the close needs to do what it can to make the return to the workplace as positive as possible. The employee who slinks out with shoulders slumped and spirit humbled may satisfy the occasional bloodthirsty manager, but will not help a poised and self-confident return to work.

Follow-up

(a) Record

Except for the most informal encounters a record of the discussion has to be made by the manager, not only to have a note of what should happen, but also for procedural reasons:

> After the disciplinary interview is over, it is essential to record both the fact that it has taken place and a synopsis of what transpired. Thus if the interviewee has been officially reminded during the interview that the consequences of further offences will have to be considered in terms of the further stages of a disciplinary procedure . . . he should be given a copy of a permanent record of the fact that this was said. (Hackett, 1981, p. 154)

Even when the juggernaut of procedure is not involved, there is still value in noting what was agreed in order to reduce the likelihood of a difficult matter being conveniently forgotten.

(b) Action

Something must happen after the interview. Some managers seem to believe that it is enough to demonstrate that they were right, rather like getting the better of someone who challenges you to a duel; but the point of the exercise is not to prove you were right, it is to bring about a change in the working performance of the respondent. There is also the possibility that interviews in procedure result in the matter going further as the respondent appeals against what has been said and any penalty that may have been given. If there is an appeal the importance of the written record becomes even greater.

(c) Review

Some time after the interview the matter has to be reviewed to see what has changed. Has the problem been overcome or is there still a difficulty? If all is well there may be a need to review any warnings, especially formal warnings, that the employee may have received, as procedure often includes provisions for 'cleaning the slate' of an employee who has been in trouble but manages to put matters right after a trouble-free period. The last aspect of review is to consider disciplinary problems in aggregate. If certain types of problem occur frequently with different people, there is need for further investigation. Also, rules need regular review to ensure that they relate to current aspects of operations rather than those that are obsolete. Recently, a small brewery reprinted its works rules, containing several instructions to employees about horse-drawn vehicles but none about motorized vehicles, although they have not used horses for thirty years.

Table 11.1 *The discipline sequence*

Preparation
1. Check:
   - the procedural position;
   - the availability of the evidence;
   - who will be present.
2. Ensure that the location of the interview is appropriate.

Encounter
1. Explain the management position.
2. Find out the employee position.
3. Examine the problem.
4. If the problem has not been resolved try the following:
   (a) persuasion;
   (b) disapproval;
   (c) penalties.

Follow-up
1. Record:
   - what happened;
   - agreed action.
2. Take any action necessary.
3. File interview notes for later review.

References

Department of Employment (1973) *In Working Order: a study of industrial discipline*, HMSO, London.

Edwards, P. K. (1989) 'The three faces of discipline', in K. Sisson (ed.), *Personnel Management in Britain*, Blackwell, Oxford.

Hackett, P. (1981) *Interview Skills Training*, 2nd edn, Institute of Personnel Management, London.

Huberman, J. (1964) 'Discipline without punishment', *Harvard Business Review*, vol. 42, no. 4 (August), pp. 62–8.

Salamon, M.W. (1987) *Industrial Relations: Theory and practice*, Prentice Hall, Hemel Hempstead.

Tietjen, T. (1987) *I'd Like a Word with You*, Video Arts, London.

Torrington, D. P. and L. A. Hall, (1987) *Personnel Management: A new approach*, Prentice Hall, Hemel Hempstead.

Exercise 11

In the booklet *I'd Like to Have a Word With You* (1987), Tina Tietjen identifies ten categories of difficult respondent in disciplinary interviews. One of these is 'the professional weeper' (Figure 11.3):

> This is the person who can turn on tears like turning on a tap. Some people are quite umoved by tears, but lots of bosses find tears and emotion very hard to cope with. They are either very embarrassed or very apologetic that their words could have had such an effect. (Tietjen, 1987, p.26)

Figure 11.3 *The professional weeper*

Another is 'the counter-attacker', who

> operates on the maxim that the best defence is attack. Once you have stated your reasons for the interview, he will leap straight into the discussion, relishing the opportunity to 'have it out'. The obvious danger is that you respond to his aggression, that a battle of words will ensue and that nothing else will happen. (p. 28)

How would you respond to the professional weeper? Can you recall a situation when you have had to cope with tears and emotion? How will you do it next time?

How would you respond to the counter-attacker? Do you find it difficult to avoid rising to the bait of being drawn into an argument? How will you do it next time?

12 Problem-solving: The appraisal interview

Performance appraisal is the number one American management problem. It takes the average employee (manager or non-manager) six months to recover from it. (Peters, 1989; p. 495).

There are many appraisal schemes being designed and implemented in all areas of employment. Once installed, schemes are frequently being modified or abandoned and there is widespread management frustration about their operation.

The following extracts are taken from answers written by students of the Institute of Personnel Management, taking professional examinations in the summer of 1989:

> Our scheme has been abandoned because of a lot of paperwork to be completed by the manager and the time-consuming nature of the preparation by both appraiser and appraisee. Assessment dragged on from week to week without any tangible outcome, there was no follow-up and few people understood the process. The interview was spent with managers talking generalities and appraisees having nothing to say. (From a large engineering company.)

> We have had approximately one new scheme per year over the last six years. These have ranged from a blank piece of paper to multi-form exercises, complete with tick-boxes and a sentence of near death if they were not complete by a specified date. (From an international motor manufacturer.)

> Our scheme is not objective and has become a meaningless ritual. It is not a system of annual appraisal; it is an annual handicap. (From a public corporation.)

Despite the problems, the potential advantages of appraisal are so great that organizations continue to introduce them and they can produce stunning results. Here is another extract from the same set of examination answers:

> I have had annual appraisal for three years. Each time it has been a searching discussion of my objectives and my results. Each interview has set me new challenges and opened up fresh opportunities. Appraisal has given me a sense of achievement and purpose that I had never previously experienced in my working life. (From an insurance company.)

There are two contrasted views of appraisal: the control approach and the development approach. Both types are found, with the control being the most common, especially when there is a link with performance-related pay, but the alternative development emphasis is gaining in popularity. Increasingly, appraisal schemes have elements of both approaches, but describing them as polar opposites helps to illustrate the key elements.

1. *The control approach* starts with an expression of opinion by someone 'up there', representing the view of controlling, responsible authority in saying:'We must stimulate effective performance and develop potential, set targets to be achieved, reward above-average achievement and ensure that promotion is based on sound criteria.'

Despite its specious appeal (after all, it is perfectly reasonable), that type of initiative is almost always resisted by people acting collectively, either by representation through union machinery or through passive resistance and grudging participation. This is because people whose performance will be appraised construe the message in a way that is not usually intended by the controlling authorities, like this:

> They will put pressure on poor performers so that they improve or leave. They will also make sure that people do what they're told and we will all be vulnerable to individual managerial whim and prejudice, losing a bit more control over our individual destinies.

It is the most natural human reaction to be apprehensive about judgements that will be made about you by other people, however good their intentions.

This approach is likely to engender the following:

1. Conflictual behaviour and attitudes within the organization, including resistance by managers to the amount of administrative work involved in the process.
2. Negotiated modifications to schemes. These are 'concessions'

made to ease the apprehension of people who feel vulnerable. These frequently make the schemes ineffective.

3. Tight bureaucratic controls to ensure consistency and fairness of reported judgements.
4. Bland, safe statements in the appraisal process.
5. Little impact on actual performance, except on that of a minority of self-assured high achievers at one extreme and disenchanted idlers at the other.
6. Reduced openness, trust and initiative.

It works best when there are clear and specific targets for people to reach, within an organizational culture that emphasizes competition. There are considerable problems, like who sets the standards and who makes the judgements? How are the judgements, by different appraisers of different appraisees, made consistent? Despite its drawbacks, this approach is still potentially useful as a system of keeping records and providing a framework for career development that is an improvement on references and panel interviews. It is most appropriate in bureaucratic organizations. The emphasis is on *form-filling*.

Appraisal is valueless unless the general experience of it is satisfactory. Appraisees have to find some value in the appraisal process itself and have to see tangible outcomes in follow-up. Appraisers have to find the appraisal process not too arduous and have to see constructive responses from appraisees. When general experience of appraisal is satisfactory, it becomes an integral part of managing the organization and modifies the management process.

2. *The development approach* starts with the question in the mind of the individual job holder:'I am not sure whether I am doing a good job or not. I would like to find ways of doing the job better, if I can, and I would like to clarify and improve my career prospects.' This question is addressed by job holders *to themselves*. Not 'Please sir, am I doing what you want?', but:

> Where can I find someone to talk through with me my progress, my hopes, my fears. Who can help me come to terms with my limitations and understand my mistakes? Where can I find someone with the experience and wisdom to discuss my performance with me so that I can shape it, building on my strengths to improve the fit between what I can contribute and what the organization needs from me?

Those in positions of authority tend to put a slightly different construction on this approach, which is something like: 'This leads to people doing what they want to do rather than what they should be doing. There is no co-ordination, no comparison and no satisfactory management control.'

This approach to appraisal does the following:

1. Develops co-operative behaviour between appraisers and appraisees and encourages people to exercise self-discipline, accepting autonomous responsibility.
2. Confronts issues, seeking to resolve problems.
3. Does not work well with bureaucratic control.
4. Produces searching analysis directly affecting performance.
5. Requires high trust, engenders loyalty and stimulates initiative.

It works best with people who are professionally self-assured, so that they can generate constructive criticism in discussion with a peer; or in protégé–mentor situations, where there is high mutual respect. The emphasis is on *interviewing*, rather than on form-filling. Despite the benefits of this approach, there are two problems: first is the lack of the systematic reporting that is needed for attempts at management control of, and information about, the process; second is the problem of everyone finding a paragon in whom they can trust.

Review topic 12.1

To what extent can the benefits of both approaches be created in a single scheme?
  Who should conduct the appraisal interview?

Despite the problems, the potential advantages of performance appraisal are so great that attempts are made to make it work. Among the reasons why 'seniors' may wish to appraise 'juniors' in an organization are the following:

- *Human-resources considerations*: to ensure the abilities and energies of individuals are being effectively used and that skills or aptitudes are not being neglected if there is scope for their better use.

- *Training*: identifying training needs so the contribution of individuals may be developed.

- *Promotion*: appraisal can assist decision-making in promotion, although direct links between appraisal and promotion are rare.

- *Planning:* to identify skill shortages and succession needs.

- *Authority:* appraisal sustains the hierarchy of authority by confirming the dependence of subordinates on those who carry out the appraisals.

Among the reasons why 'juniors' may wish to be appraised by their 'seniors' in an organization are the following:

- *Performance:* one's ability to do the job may be enhanced by an emphasis on strengths and an understanding of what changes are needed

- *Motivation:* reassurance can increase the level of enthusiasm and commitment to the job.

- *Career:* individuals can get guidance and indicators about possible job changes.

Review topic 12.2

Are there any other reasons you can add to either of those lists?

There are, however, many problems for those carrying out the appraisal, for example:

- *Prejudice:* the appraiser may actually be prejudiced against the appraisee, or be anxious not to be prejudiced; either could distort the appraiser's judgement.

- *Insufficient knowledge of the appraisee:* appraisers often carry out appraisals because of their position in the hierarchy rather than because they have a good understanding of what the appraisee is doing.

- *The 'halo effect':* the general likeability (or the opposite) of an appraisee can influence the assessment of the work that the appraisee is doing.

- *The problem of context:* the difficulty of distinguishing the work of appraisees from the context in which they work, especially when there is an element of comparison with other appraisees.

Review topic 12.3

Think of jobs where it is difficult to disentangle the performance of the individual from the context of the work. How would you focus on the individual's performance in these situations?

Problems for both the appraiser and the appraisee include the following:

- *The paperwork:* documentation soon gets very cumbersome in the attempts made by scheme designers to ensure consistent reporting.

- *The formality:* although appraisers are likely to try and avoid stiff formality, both participants in the interview realize that the encounter is relatively formal, with much hanging on it.

Among the other common problems that often cause appraisal schemes to fail are:

- *Outcomes are ignored:* follow-up action agreed in the interview for management to take fails to take place.

- *Everyone is 'just above average':* most appraisees are looking for reassurance that all is well, and the easiest way for appraisers to deal with this is by a statement or inference that the appraiser is doing at least as well as most others, and better than a good many (Figure 12.1). It is much harder to deal with the situation of facing someone with the opinion that they are average – who wants to be average?

- *Appraising the wrong features:* sometimes behaviours other than the real work are evaluated, such as time-keeping, looking busy and being pleasant, because they are easier to see.

The problem-solving approach to the appraisal interview is the most effective, providing that both the appraiser and appraisee have the skill and ability to handle this mode. This approach is similar to counselling, as neither of the parties knows 'the answer' before the interview begins: it develops by the process of interaction itself.

This is not the only type of appraisal interview. Norman Maier (1976) identified two main alternatives. *Tell and sell* is where the appraiser acts as judge, using the interview to tell the appraisee the result of the interview and how to improve. This 'ski-instructor' approach can be appropriate when the appraisees have little experience and have not developed enough self-confidence to analyse their own performance. *Tell and listen* still casts the appraiser

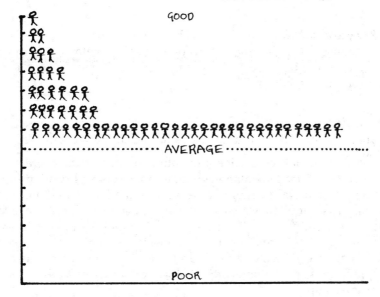

EMPLOYEE PERFORMANCE CHART 1990

Figure 12.1 *Just above average*

in the role of judge, passing on the outcome of an appraisal that has already been completed and listening to reactions. These could sometimes change the assessment, as well as enabling the two to have a reasonably frank exchange.

The appraisal sequence

Preparation

(a) Appraisee briefing

Brief the appraisee on the form of the interview, possibly asking for a self-appraisal form to be completed in readiness. To some extent this is establishing rapport in advance, with the same objectives, and makes the opening of the eventual interview easier.

Asking for the self-appraisal form to be completed will only be appropriate if the scheme requires this. Self-appraisal is currently popular, on the basis that it gives the appraisee some initiative, ensures that the discussion will be about matters which the appraisee can handle and on 'real stuff'. There is, however, useful research evidence that appraisees in this situation typically overestimate their own achievements and potential (Makin and Robertson, 1983).

(b) Appraiser briefing

The appraiser reviews all the available evidence on the appraisee's performance, including reports, records or other material regarding the period under review. Most important will be the previous appraisal and its outcomes.

Encounter

(a) Rapport

Rapport is unusual because it is attempting to smoothe the interaction between two people who probably have an easy social relationship, but now find themselves ill at ease with each other. This is not the sort of conversation they are used to having together, so they have to find new ground rules. The pre-interview appraisee briefing is an important step towards this, but the opening of the interview itself still needs care. The mood needs to be light, but not trivial, as the appraisee has to be encouraged towards candour rather than gamesmanship.

Review topic 12.4

What do you think of the following openings to appraisal interviews heard recently:

1. 'Well, here we are again. I'm sure you don't like this business any more than I do, so let's get on with it.'
2. 'Now, there's nothing to worry about. It's quite painless and could be useful. So just relax and let me put a few questions to you.'
3. 'I wonder if I will end up conning you more than you will succeed in conning me.'
4. 'Right. Let battle commence.'

(b) Factual review

The sequence is very similar to that for counselling. Begin by reviewing the main facts about the performance, without expressing opinions about them but merely summarizing them as a mutual reminder. This will include the outcome of the previous appraisal.

(c) Positive reinforcement

The appraiser will still be doing most – but not all – of the talking, and will now isolate those aspects of performance that have been disclosed which are clearly satisfactory, mention them and comment favourably. This will provide the basic reassurance that the appraisee needs in order to avoid being defensive. The favourable aspects of performance will be taken from the factual review, to some extent being discovered by the factual review process. Not, 'Well, I think you are getting on very well. I'm very pleased with how things are going generally.' That sort of comment made at this stage would have the appraisee waiting for 'but . . . ', as the defences have not yet been dismantled. A different approach might be, 'Those figures are pretty good . . . . How do they compare with . . .? That's x per cent up on the quarter and y per cent on the year . . . . That's fine . . . . You must be pleased with that . . . . How on earth did you do it?' This has the advantage of the evidence being there before the eyes of both parties, with the appraiser pointing out and emphasizing; and it is specific rather than general, precise rather than vague. If there is not some feature of the performance that can be isolated in this way, then the appraiser probably has a management or disciplinary problem that should have been tackled earlier.

(d) Appraisee questions

The appraiser then asks for the appraisee's comments on things that are not as good as they might be in the performance, areas of possible improvement and how these might be addressed. These will only be offered by the appraisee if there has been effective positive re-inforcement. People can only acknowledge shortcomings about performance when they are reasonably sure of their ground. Now the appraisee is examining areas of dissatisfaction by the process of discussing them with the appraiser, with whom it is worth having the discussion, because of the appraiser's expertise, information and helicopter view (Figure 12.2). There are three likely results of debating these matters:

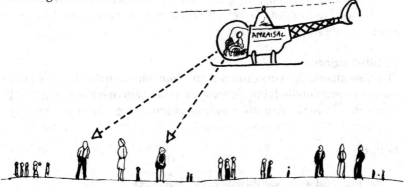

Figure 12.2 *Helicopter view*

- Some will be talked out as baseless.

- Some will be shown to be less worrying than they seemed when viewed only from the single perspective of the appraiser, and ways of dealing with them become apparent.

- Some will be confirmed as matters needing attention.

This stage in the interview is fraught with difficulties for the manager: 'some employees prefer to be told rather than invited to participate . . . the manager receives extra pay and status for making decisions, so why should the manager expect them to do his or her job as well?' (Wright and Taylor, 1984, p. 110). These, however, are problems to be recognized and overcome; they are not reasons for not bothering to try.

(e) Appraiser comments

Now the appraiser adds to the list of areas for improvement. In many instances there will be no additions to make, but usually there are improvement needs that the appraisee cannot, or will not, see. If they are put at this point in the interview, there is the best chance that they will be understood, accepted and acted upon. It is not possible to guarantee success. Demoralized collapse or bitter resentment is always a possibility, but this is the time to try, as the appraisee has developed a basis of reassurance and has come to terms with some shortcomings that he or she had already recognized.

The appraiser has to judge whether any further issues can be raised and if so, how many. None of us can cope with confronting all our shortcomings, all at the same time, and the appraiser's underlying management responsibility is that the appraisee is not made less competent by the appraisal interview. There is also a fundamental moral responsibility not to use a position of organizational power to damage the self-esteem and adjustment of another human being.

Only when you have a very high degree of mutual trust can you afford to mix step (c) with step (d).

(f) Joint action

The final stage of the encounter is to agree what is to be done. As with the other problem-solving interviews, it is likely that some action will be needed from the appraiser as well as some from the appraisee.

Follow-up

1. Record problems identified and action agreed.
2. Take action on appraiser points.
3. File interview notes for later review.

Table 12.1 *The appraisal sequence*

Preparation
1. Check:
   - appraisee briefing;
   - appraiser briefing.
   (Possibly ask for self-appraisal to be completed.)

Encounter
1. Begin with:
   - rapport.
2. Develop through four stages of:
   - factual review;
   - positive reinforcement;
   - appraisee questions;
   - appraiser comments.
3. Agree:
   - joint action.

Follow-up
1. Record problems and agreed action.
2. Take action on appraiser points.
3. File interview notes for later review.

References

Maier, N.R.F. (1976) *The Appraisal Interview: Three basic approaches*, University Associates, La Jolla, CA.

Makin P. and I.T. Robertson (1983) 'Self assessment, realistic job previews and occupational decisions', *Personnel Review*, 12 (3), pp. 21–5.

Peters T. (1989) *Thriving on Chaos*, Pan Books, London.

Wright P.L. and D.S. Taylor (1984) *Improving Leadership Performance*, Prentice Hall, Hemel Hempstead.

Exercise 12a

Again you need a colleague to work with, but the exercise requires less soul-bearing than counselling, so it can be effective with someone you know only slightly. You take turns to interview the other. The aim is to talk real stuff about your respective jobs. One of you is A, the other is B.

1. Preparation by A:
   Write down the response to the following questions on separate cards or pieces of paper.

(a) An activity you perform in your job that is very important (this should begin with a verb, e.g. 'carrying out appraisal interviews' not a role or responsibility).

(b) An activity you do frequently – not necessarily important, but one which occupies a good deal of time.

(c) An activity, though important, unlikely to appear in your diary.

(d) What is the most important activity not so far listed?

2. Interview/discussion led by B on above topics:

- How are (a) and (b) similar, and how are they different?
- What makes them easier, or harder, to do than (c)?
- Which is it more important in your job to do well, (b) or (c)?
- On what criteria did you select (d)?
- Which gives you most satisfaction, (a),(b),(c) or (d)?

Now change roles.

Exercise 12b

Having begun the process of examining what you do with a colleague, you now move on to a similar exercise in which you have a different type of structure. It is a mini-appraisal, in which you interview each other about work done in the first week of the month.

1. A interviews B for information about A's week. (15 minutes)
2. B interviews A for information about B's week. (15 minutes)
3. A and B prepare for feedback and discussion. (15 minutes)
4. B conducts appraisal interview with A about the week. (30 minutes +)
5. A conducts appraisal interview with B about the week. (30 minutes +)
6. A and B discuss with each other what they liked and disliked about the process.

Points to remember:
The first interview is for information gathering.

The second interview is for feedback. This should include opport-unities for positive reinforcement. Only criticize with care.

A final discussion could consider the questions: 'How useful did you find it to discuss an aspect of your work with someone who was well informed, but not your "boss"?' 'Would it have been more or less useful having that discussion with your boss?'

13 Conflict resolution: Negotiation

Negotiation has become more commonplace as other methods of settling arguments have become impracticable. In international affairs, warfare between states has been partly replaced by negotiation; terrorism has introduced negotiation as a necessary method of dealing with hijackers and others who have taken hostages; and complicated business deals proliferate.

In employment we have collective bargaining as a means of regulating the employment relationship between employer and organized employees. To some this is the cornerstone of industrial democracy and the effective running of a business, but others see it as a poor substitute for executive action, impairing efficiency, inhibiting change and producing the lowest, rather than the highest, common factor of co-operation between management and employees.

Although a long-standing art, negotiation has developed as a major mode of decision-making in all aspects of organizational life. The more sophisticated features of selling and purchasing involve extensive negotiation, which are more than simply haggling about price. There are dealings with revenue representatives, bank officials, as well as the inevitable internal management struggles.

Is negotiation rightly viewed as an activity that is only second best to unilateral decision? If the outcome is no more than a compromise, then negotiation may be the recourse of no alternative other than capitulation. In that situation some would argue that capitulation by one side would be a better outcome for both than a compromise that smudges the difficulties and dissatisfies both parties.

There is, however, an alternative in negotiation to simply splitting the difference. The negotiating process itself makes clear the differences in objectives between the parties to an extent that cannot be achieved by other means. It then proceeds to find ways of accommodating those conflicting aims to achieve an outcome that is better for both than could have been achieved by the unilateral executive action of either.

More than compromise

Any negotiation is brought about by the existence of goals that are common to both parties and goals that conflict. If the Americans and the Russians had not had at least one common goal (to reduce the risk of nuclear holocaust) the talks to find agreement between the two countries on the limitation of strategic arms could not have taken place; if they had not had a number of conflicting goals, the talks would not have been necessary. Between employer and employees the desire to keep the business in operation is one of the goals they usually have in common, but there may be many that conflict, and the two parties negotiate a settlement because the attempt by one to force a solution on the other would either fail because of the other's strength or would not be a workable solution without the willing compliance of the other party.

Both parties acknowledge that they will move from their opening position and that sacrifices in one area may produce more-than-compensating benefits in another. Many years ago the American, Homans expressed the situation thus:

> The more the items at stake can be divided into goods valued more by one party than they cost to the other and goods valued more by the other party than they cost to the first, the greater the chances of a successful outcome. (Homans, 1961, p. 62)

Another limited view of negotiation is that the encounter is merely to disclose what each party wants from the other, and that the outcome can be predicted beforehand: 'They will ask for 10 per cent . . . .. We will say "no" and six weeks later we'll settle for 5 per cent.' Where that happens the negotiations are locked into a pattern of no more than compromise, whereas they should be approached as a process that shapes the outcome, as the parties explore possibilities of integrating their conflicting objectives. This can be a long, time-consuming process, it is often accompanied by acrimony and mistrust, but it is a way of introducing significant change and overcoming problems that cannot be dealt with as well by other means, providing that the nature of the process is understood:

> negotiators seek to increase common interest and expand
> cooperation in order to broaden the area of agreement to cover the
> item under dispute. On the other hand, each seeks to maximize his
> own interest and prevail in conflict, in order to make the agreement
> more valuable to himself. No matter what angle analysis takes, it
> cannot eliminate the basic tension between cooperation and conflict
> that provides the dynamic of negotiation. (Zartman, 1976, p. 41)

Review topic 13.1

Scan through your newspaper today to spot reports of negotiations on any subject – international affairs, a business deal, an industrial dispute or attempts to forge a political alliance. In which are the differences between the parties being resolved, and in which are they being accommodated?

The main work on understanding the interpersonal dynamics of the negotiating process is by Ann Douglas (1962), which has been the basis of more recent work in the United Kingdom by Morley and Stephenson (1970, 1977), Brotherton and Stephenson (1975) and Kniveton and Towers (1978). A complementary strand of analysis was developed by Walton and McKersie (1965) as well as a rather different approach by Walton in 1969. In all of these we find an approach to negotiation as a constructive process, whereby differences between parties are openly confronted in working towards an accommodation to provide a degree of satisfaction for both parties which is greater than can be achieved either by simple compromise or by the 'victory' of one at the expense of the other.

The bargaining setting

Negotiating is such a specialized activity that it needs appropriate circumstances to make a productive outcome likely.

(a) Resolution or accommodation?

The parties in negotiation are confronting differences between them: dealing with conflict. This is not necessarily bitter and combative, but it is a divergence within the co-operative framework. That may be resolved, in which case the original feelings of opposition disappear and the relationship between the parties becomes one of co-operation without any element of conflict. This has obvious attractions and many people feel that negotiation has failed if resolution is not achieved. However, many of the matters negotiated in the field of industrial relations are those where a conflict of interest is inevitable. Management representatives are mainly seeking efficiency, cost-effectiveness, productivity and the obedience of others to their own authority. Employee representatives are seeking high pay, freedom of action, leisure and scope for the individual. To some extent it is inevitable that these will conflict, so resolution of conflict may seldom be achieved. More realistic is an accommodation between diverging interests; the differences persist, but a way of living with them is found. This sounds like an unambitious objective, but an accommodation can still introduce major change in the workplace and a new situation which is both better than the one it replaced and better than could have been achieved by the unilateral action of the management. Negotiators need to consider the alternatives in their initial target-setting and decide which they are hoping to attain.

(b) The balance of power

Negotiations only begin because each party has some power over the other. Naturally, each team of negotiators wants to be the one with the power advantage, but it is doubtful if this helps them. If there is an imbalance of power it is difficult for both parties to be frank and to trust what is said by the other. The weaker party will be defensive and suspicious, lacking the confidence of having some room for manoeuvre. The stronger party will feel inhibited from destroying the opposition. The best situation is where there is an equality of power between the two. 'Effective negotiation is rarely limited to the sheer exploitation of power advantage. The best settlement is one in which both sides can recognise their own and mutual advantages' (Fowler, 1986, p. 132).

In the ebb and flow of economic prosperity there come times when management have considerable power in relation to their employees and are in a position to say 'no' to claims without too much fear of short-term inconvenience in industrial action. Usually they take advantage of such situations to bring about changes despite employee reluctance, and often economic stringency leaves them with no alternative. On other occasions the employees' union representatives are in a position to make substantial demands because their position is relatively stronger and the management have less freedom of action. Only a dreamy idealist would argue that the party with a power advantage should not use it when they see the opportunity, but the short-term gain may become a long-term handicap: revenge is sweet.

The argument that power parity is most conducive to success in negotiations only holds while there is a negotiating relationship. Managements may be able to use periods of the odds being in their favour to remove some matters from negotiation altogether. Short-sighted managements may also use that as an opportunity to reduce the degree of mutual advantage.

(c) Tension level and synchronizing

A negotiating approach by one party to the other is best made when the other party is ready to deal with it. Managers often resort to negotiation only when there is no alternative due to a crisis having developed, making a negotiated solution the only possible outcome. If it is not a propitious time for the employees, their response may be grudging or ill-prepared, involving procrastination. The next time the management may not be prepared for an employee initiative, with similar results.

The timing of most negotiations is dictated by extraneous factors rather than the inclinations of the negotiators, but those involved have some influence on the timing of encounters and may be able to push them towards a time of mutual readiness. One aspect of appropriate timing is the level of tension that exists. If this is too low there is no real will to reach a settlement so that negotiators do not have the impetus to grapple with difficult questions. If there is too much tension, there is so much anxiety that negotiators cannot see issues clearly and become preoccupied with interpersonal wrangling and vilification. If negotiations can take place when both sides have a balanced desire to reach a settlement, this can be as helpful as a balance of power.

The negotiation sequence

Ritual is especially important as negotiation is a specialized activity and its conflictual base makes for formality and awkwardness rather than relaxed, informal behaviours. All confrontations have strong ritual features. The international tennis player 'shows' the new balls to the opponent even though they both watched them being produced from the box; in some Arab countries it is impossible to make any major purchase without drinking tea; in the nineteenth century duels between young aristocrats were fought according to a most elaborate set of rules. Management–employee negotiations are also full of ritual steps:

> guided (where it is not merely a spontaneous response to
> perception of self-interest) either by tradition, custom or habit, or
> by a set of norms and rules which, in so far as they are coherent for
> a particular kind of action, may be regarded as the rules of a distinct
> game. (Thomason, 1984, p. 328)

This infuriates some newcomers to negotiation, who see it as time-wasting prevarication; but it is an inescapable feature of the process, even though it may not be a feature of other similar activities like consultation and providing information. The rituals make a structured approach to negotiating, in the manner of this book, particularly appropriate.

Preparation

(a) Agenda

The agenda can affect both the conduct and outcome of the negotiations. It influences the conduct of the encounter by revealing and delimiting the matters that each side wants to deal with. It is unlikely that other matters will be added to the agenda, particularly if negotiations take place regularly between the parties, so the negotiators begin to see, before the meeting, what form the discussions can take.

The sequence of items on the agenda will influence the outcome of negotiations as the scope for accommodation between the two positions emerges in the discussions. If, for instance, all the items of the employees' claim come first and all the management's points come later, possibilities do not turn into probabilities until the discussions are well advanced. An agenda which juxtaposes management and employee 'points' in a logical fashion can enable the shape of a settlement to develop in the minds of the negotiators earlier, even though there would be no commitment until all the pieces of the jigsaw were available.

Many negotiations take place without an agenda at all, sometimes because there is a crisis, sometimes because neither party is sufficiently well organized to prepare one and sometimes because the party initiating the negotiations believes there is a tactical advantage in surprising the opponent. Morley and Stephenson (1977, pp. 74–8) review a number of studies to draw the conclusion that agreement between negotiators is facilitated when there is the opportunity for them to experience 'orientation' considering on what to stand firm and on what to contemplate yielding – or an understanding of the issues involved. An agenda is a prerequisite of orientation.

(b) Information and objectives

Although negotiations sometimes seem to be nothing but opposed opinions and heated exchanges between strong personalities, the currency of the exchanges and the basis on which a case is made or refuted is information, so negotiators prepare by marshalling and mastering data. Information is needed firstly to understand the situation and the issues that are the subject of negotiation, and secondly to review the party's position – its strengths and weaknesses. This may throw up the need for further information. When it is all collected the negotiating team meet to ensure they share the same interpretation of that information.

Negotiators' objectives will be partly described by the agenda, and collecting and sharing an interpretation of the relevant information may have to precede work on the agenda to make sure that it reflects correctly what the negotiators are trying to achieve.

Seldom do management negotiators work out useful objectives. This may be due to a distaste for the whole bargaining activity, but often it is because the only outcome they can foresee is to lose something, and their objective is to lose as little as possible. In recent years the question 'What do you seek to achieve in the forthcoming negotiations?' has been put to those entering both real and laboratory-type negotiations. Seldom does the answer do more than reflect vague values:

- 'Assert management athority.'
- 'Get the best deal we can.'
- 'Hope that reason will prevail.'

and the ubiquitous,

- 'Play it by ear.'

When negotiators can approach negotiations with objectives that are more than a simple negation of what is sought by the other side, there is the chance of reaching a mutually satisfactory agreement. Otherwise there is scope for little but mutual attrition.

Not all objectives will be achieved, but their reality will be improved by predicting the counter-claims. This is not simply what is on the agenda as topics for discussion, but the nature and expected strength of the arguments that will be heard. If a team of negotiators can guess what will be said to them, they may well be able to restructure their objectives to stand a better chance of success. This does not necessarily mean seeking less, but it probably does mean seeking differently: possibly more.

Review topic 13.2

Remember your scan through today's newspaper in review topic 13.1? What evidence is there in any of the reports that the negotiations would have been more satisfactory for both sides if there had been better information available to the parties?

(c) The negotiating team

The attention of all negotiators will be directed towards handling the differences between the parties. Differences within parties are a nuisance, so that the team that is not united not only serves poorly the interests of those they represent, the time of those they oppose is also wasted, as the opponents do not know who is to be relied on. It is therefore important that the members of each team agree among themselves first, so that the two opposed sets of interests can be accurately confronted.

Atkinson (1977, pp. 87–9) suggests that there are three basic functions of a bargaining team – negotiating, recording and analysing – and that teams should comprise people to handle these separately. Another way of looking at team composition is to consider the roles of the participants, while accepting that there are quite different activities to be undertaken. The major role is *leading advocate*. This person will set out the team's case on each succeeding point, examine the opposing case and make a series of on-the-spot judgements about when to introduce new material, change tack and all the other decisions that shape the quality and direction of the encounter. The advocate has the lion's share of the negotiating task to perform, and is likely to be the person with the most status among the team members. If seen to be clearly out-ranked by another member of the team, there is a tendency for the opposing team to appeal to this more senior member, thereby undermining the effectiveness of the advocate and the cohesion of the team.

The *specialist* is the team member who does not lead, but who deals with particular points of information and analysis. In talks on payment arrangements, for instance, there may be a specialist to answer questions and provide facts about how the existing pay scheme works, or to correct false impressions that may be claimed. There may be several specialists, or some who come only for certain phases of the negotiation. They are not involved directly in the debate and negotiations are not helped by the single shop steward who advances a separate line of argument, nor by the manager who begins to make points that detract from, rather than support, the case that is being mounted by the management advocate. Negotiating does not benefit from free-for-all, unstructured discussion.

There is no need for all those present to speak. There is a valuable part to be played by those who simply *observe*, as they have two advantages over other participants: firstly they do not suffer the same degree of agitation and hurt that attends those who suffer the 'slings and arrows' of heated argument; secondly, they do not have to cope with the job of preparing what they are going to say and making their entry into the dialogue. That means that they hear more of what is said on both sides and are able to assess developments more dispassionately than the advocate, who is too busy, and the specialist, who is interested more in one aspect than others. During adjournments it is the observers who can best initiate discussion among team members as strategy is redefined and further tactics considered. They can also record proceedings, although it is often only the outcome that is worth recording rather than the discussions themselves. Observers are most conveniently people of equal or junior rank to advocates and specialists. When someone attends who is perceived as a potential overrider of decisions or knocker-together of disagreeing heads, it makes the negotiations a hollow process if that observer never speaks.

A possible additional role is that of *chairman*. The logic here is clear, but the practice usually different. Logically, one cannot act simultaneously as judge and counsel for the prosecution, so that one person is needed to chair the discussion and control the meeting, while another engages in advocacy. In practice, most negotiations seem not to need chairing, because the proceedings are discussion or argument rather than debate. There is a fairly rapid change of speakers from one side of the table to another, usually involving only one person, so that chairing becomes irrelevant. In larger, complex negotiations it is more common to find a chairman. Usually it is a member of the management, other than the advocate, sometimes there is a convention that the chairmanship alternates between the two sides.

Occasionally, negotiations have an independent mediator between the two sides, who will also chair any meetings that take place during the mediation process.

Encounter

(a) Setting
We saw in Chapter 2 that there is a preference for face-to-face orientation between people who are engaged in a competitive task. Negotiations are best conducted when the seating arrangements divide the parties clearly, as this focuses the attention of everyone on the issues dividing them, as it is these that have to be understood, juxtaposed and eventually accommodated. Other aspects of seating arrangements are summarized by Kniveton and Towers (1978, p. 56): 'participants vary in status and tend to select positions which reflect this status. Secondly, the position selected affects the influence the member has over the meeting, and thirdly, the seating arrangements affect the flow of communication.'

The highest-status people in each team would normally be in the middle (Figure 13.1), although Kniveton and Towers make the interesting comment that a principal negotiator hoping to dominate the meeting would tend to take the head of the table, but would take a different position when wanting the other side to take the initiative.

Figure 13.1 *The highest-status people in each team are normally in the middle*

The number of people taking part in negotiations has two main influences: the first is in the preparatory discussions, when strategy is being formulated and cohesion being developed; the second is in the negotiating encounter itself. Slater (1958) conducted experiments from which he concluded that the optimum size for discussions of the type that precede negotiation is five. If there are fewer, group members may feel that they lack variety or expertise or do not discuss the issue forthrightly because of an overwhelming desire to be nice to each other. If there are more, the scope for individual participation is reduced by the number of competing voices.

In negotiations themselves the number of active, vocal participants will be less, but everyone will be communicating in some way, even if only by periodically raising their eyebrows or biting their nails, so the more people that are present the more there is a tendency to a distant type of formality and a puzzling variety of cues about the reactions of the other team.

Because of their public nature there are innumerable examples from international political negotiations of the difficulty that the setting can present. Winston Churchill described how there were two levels of activity at the Teheran meeting between himself, Roosevelt and Stalin towards the end of the Second World War. There were plenary sessions with thirty people present and 'three-only' meetings between himself, Roosevelt and Stalin, with interpreters. It needed meetings of both types to make progress. The start of the Vietnam peace talks in Paris twenty years later was delayed for three weeks because of an inability among the negotiators to agree on the shape of the table! One of the most beguiling examples is quoted by Morley and Stephenson (1970, pp. 22–3) from Harold Macmillan describing a 1955 summit meeting:

> The room in which we met filled me with horror the moment we entered it. The protagonists were sitting at tables drawn up in a rectangle; the space between them was about the size of a small boxing ring. But this arena was itself surrounded by rows of benches and seats which were provided, presumably, for the advisers, but seemed to be occupied by a crowd of interested onlookers. The walls were decorated with vast, somewhat confused, frescoes, depicting the end of the world, or the Battle of the Titans, or the rape of the Sabines, or a mixture of all three. I could conceive of no arrangement less likely to lead to intimate or useful negotiations. The whole formal part of the conference was bound to degenerate into a series of set orations. It was only when the Heads of Government or Foreign Ministers met in a small room outside in a restricted meeting that any serious discussion could take place.

If restricted meetings of the type described by Churchill and Macmillan are required in industrial negotiations, it not only alters the character of the main negotiations, it also makes more difficult the representative role of the employee spokesmen, who may be seen as being 'in the management's pocket'.

(b) Challenge and defiance
Negotiations have three essential phases. These were identified by Ann Douglas (1962) and more recently corroborated by Morley and Stephenson (1970, 1977), working on British rather than American situations.

The first phase is described here by the melodramatic term 'challenge and defiance' to acknowledge the theatricality and quasi-warlike nature of the first ritual step in the dance. Advocates set out the position of their parties and reject the position of the other, so that by the end of this phase members of both teams should clearly understand what the issues are that divide them, why and how extensively. This differentiation is a necessary preliminary to the integration and problem-solving that follows. An important feature of the antagonism here is that it is between the parties, not between the individual negotiators. This is partly to emphasize the strength of their case, which lies in the power of those they represent. Few individual managers see themselves as being more significant and persuasive as individuals than as members of a larger body like 'the management' or 'the board', so that in most situations they add weight to their statements by alluding to their collective strength:

- The Board are right behind me on this one.'
- 'All my colleagues agree.'
- 'The management position is perfectly clear.'

Employee representatives similarly emphasize their representative role:

- 'Feeling on the shop floor is very strong.'
- 'We have a mandate from our members.'
- 'The membership has spoken.'

Another reason for the partisan emphasis is that there is a realization on both sides that they will move at some stage later – otherwise there is no point in negotiating – and the movement later can be consistent with an early assertion of absolute immovability only if the early statement is attributed to the party that is represented and the later movement is initiated by the people sitting round the table.

The other reason for this stage is a simple stiffening of the sinews and summoning up the blood, as the negotiators hear their case spelt out for the first time in public and realize how well it is organized and how just it is. They thought they were right, now they know it.

(c) Thrust and parry

After the opening show of strength the differences are known and some idea of the relative strength of the parties is beginning to form in the minds of negotiators. There is then an almost instinctive move to the next, integrative stage of the encounter. The term 'thrust and parry' is used here to describe this essentially quicker and inter-personal stage as negotiators seek out possibilities of movement and mutual accommodation. The assertive emphasis of challenge and defiance is replaced by more tentative comments, more listening and more direct response to what is being said by others. Negotiators sound out possibilities, float ideas, ask questions, make suggestions and change the style of the encounter towards a problem-solving mode. The tentative nature of the proposals is maintained by the way in which they are contrasted with what was said earlier. Challenge and defiance is 'official' and authorized by the parties. Thrust and parry is 'unofficial', without any authority – yet. Thrusts are couched in non-committal terms, specifically exonerating the party from any responsibility:

- 'My colleagues here will probably crucify me afterwards for saying this, so please don't take it as a formal offer, but suppose we could . . . '

- We have no mandate from the membership, and I don't know whether they would wear it or not, but . . . '

These behaviours are not false in the sense that negotiators are simply revealing what they have already agreed beforehand. The negotiating process itself shapes the outcome of the encounter being described here, so the non-committal behaviour of the negotiators is quite genuine as a variety of possibilities is explored.

Gradually the opportunities for mutual accommodation can be perceived in the background of the talks.

(d) Decision-making

The target point of a negotiating team is its declared objective that was spelt out so positively in challenge and defiance. The resistance point is where they would rather break off negotiations than settle. This is not declared, otherwise it would immediately become the resistance point, and it is rarely known by the negotiating team, as the point at which they would resist is seldom the same as that at which they believe they would resist. Throughout both challenge and defiance and thrust and parry the resistance points of both parties will have been moving to and fro as different possibilities become apparent. The third phase is when they reach an agreement.

It is usually up to the management to make an offer, although sometimes the employees have to take that initiative. What to offer, and when to offer it, is the single decision that is the watershed of the negotiating process and requires supreme judgement to get it right, as it has two immediate effects: firstly, it destroys the management target point, replacing it with the new offer; secondly, it will have an effect on the resistance point of the employees.

The offer may be revised, but eventually an offer is made that the employees will accept and the encounter is complete, although the negotiations are not.

Follow-up

(a) Recapitulation

When the agreement has been made the tension of the encounter is suddenly released and bargainers want nothing more than to get out of the negotiating room and spread the good news. If this temptation can be resisted, there is benefit in recapitulating the points on which agreement has been reached so as to ensure that there is no misunderstanding and to pick up any minor matters that have been overlooked. If they are picked up at this point they should be dealt with speedily because agreement is in the air. If they are left over for another meeting, they will stand on their own and may be more contentious.

Review topic 13.3

Can you recall any sort of disagreement in which you have been involved where you and the other person later disagreed about the agreement you reached to settle the matter? Was this in any way due to a lack of recapitulation?

(b) Written statement

It is foolhardy for the negotiators to split up before a written statement has been agreed. It can only be brief, and may well need to be expanded later, but if a statement is agreed before the meeting ends, then all subsequent understanding of the agreement reached – by the negotiators themselves and by others – will be based on that statement rather than word-of-mouth accounts that are likely to alter so much in the retelling. Remember how 'Send reinforcements, we are going to advance' became 'Send three and fourpence, we are going to a dance.' Until the agreement is written down, it will rest on an understanding, and understanding can easily change. There will be enough trouble in interpreting the agreement without adding to it by having a variety of agreements to interpret.

(c) Commitment of the parties

Although agreement has been reached, it is so far only between the representatives of the two parties and is of no value until and unless the parties themselves accept it and make it work. Employee representatives have to report back to their memberships and persuade them to accept the agreement which consists of something different from what was in the original mandate. Management representatives may have to do the same thing, although they customarily carry more personal authority than employee representatives.

Only when the parties are committed is the deal complete.

Table 13.1 *The negotiating sequence*

Preparation
1. Agree: agenda (content and sequence).
2. Collect: information.
3. Decide: objectives.
4. Set up: the negotiating team of:
   - advocate;
   - specialists;
   - observers;
   - (possibly a chairman).

Encounter
1. Consider: setting (seating and numbers).
2. Develop negotiations through three stages of:
   - challenge and defiance;
   - thrust and parry;
   - decision-making.

Follow-up
1. Recapitulate.
2. Produce written statement.
3. Ensure commitment of the parties.

References

Atkinson, G. G. M. (1977) *The Effective Negotiator*, Quest Research Publications, London.

Brotherton, C. J. and G. M. Stephenson (1975) 'Psychology in the system of industrial relations', *Industrial Relations Journal* (Autumn), 42–50.

Douglas, A. (1962) *Industrial Peacemaking*, Columbia University Press, New York.

Fowler, A. (1986) *Effective Negotiation*, Institute of Personnel Management London.

Homans, G. C. (1961) *Social Behaviour, Its Elementary Forms*, Routledge & Kegan Paul, London.

Kniveton, B. and B. Towers (1978) *Training for Negotiation*, Business Books, London.

Morley, I. and G. M. Stephenson (1970) 'Strength of case, communication systems, and the outcome of simulated negotiations: Some psychological aspects of bargaining', *Industrial Relations Journal*, 1 (Summer) 19–29.

Morley, I. and G. M. Stephenson (1977) *The Social Psychology of Bargaining*, Allen & Unwin, London.

Slater, P. E. (1958) 'Contrasting correlates of group size', *Sociometry*, 21, 129–39.

Thomason, G. F. (1984) *A Textbook of Industrial Relations Management*, Institute of Personnel Management, London.

Walton, R. E. (1969) *Interpersonal Peacemaking*, Addison-Wesley, Reading, MA.

Walton, R. E. and R. B. McKersie (1965) *A Behavioural Theory of Labour Negotiations*, McGraw-Hill, New York.

Zartman, I. W. (1976) *The 50% Solution*, Anchor Press/Doubleday, New York.

Exercise 13a

You again need your close friend to help you. It is probably better not to do this exercise with a spouse: either it will be hopelessly unreal, or the negotiating behaviours will be such as to subject the marriage to needless strain.

Identify a valuable possession that you might be willing to sell for a suitable price – house, car, stereo system – and that your friend might be willing to buy from you. A realistic, albeit hypothetical, willingness on both sides is a necessary feature of selecting the possession to be 'sold'. Plan your approach for negotiating the sale, including objectives, target points and resistance points. Ask your friend to carry out similar preparation as a prospective buyer.

Conduct the negotiations, attempting to avoid simple haggling about the price. When you reach potential agreement or failure to agree, discuss your feelings about the experience.

Exercise 13b

The above exercise was relatively easy, as there was only one person on each side; either party could abandon the negotiations and negotiate with someone else, and the issue in dispute was the simple question of price. Also the negotiators were representing only themselves. This next exercise gets a little nearer the real thing by involving more people and more issues, but is inevitably a more artificial situation.

You need three friends, A again to negotiate with you, B to be represented by you and C to be represented by your adversary. Although each of you is playing a role, try to avoid play-acting as far as possible. Dissuade A, for instance, from being deliberately bloody-minded and speaking with a Liverpool accent in order to play the part of a caricature shop steward.

You all need to read Document I below. Your adversary represents the TGWU members in the plant. Now continue as follows:

1. B consults with your friend C to determine three matters they would like on the agenda for a meeting with you.
2. You have similar consultations with friend B.
3. You agree an agenda for negotiations with friend A.
4. You and B finalize your objectives; A and C finalize theirs.
5. You and A conduct negotiations, while B and C observe silently and unobtrusively.*
6. You and A reach agreement, or failure to agree, and then discuss the process with B and C.

* It is important that the observers influence the progress of negotiations as little as possible. Chuckles, sharp intakes of breath and solemn shakes of the head can quickly wreck the learning experience. As far as possible observers should be out of view of the negotiators in this exercise.

Document I
You are being moved to be general manager of a subisidiary manufacturing plant that has had three different general managers in the last eight months. You have been told of the following major problems:

There is a rising rate of staff turnover on the shop floor. To maintain the complement of 420 people on production, 230 new recruits have been engaged in the last six months. In the previous six months 163 were recruited. The local level of unemployment has remained unaltered at 9 per cent.

Demand for the product fluctuates with a lead time for delivery of four to six weeks after orders are placed. You can see no possibility of smoothing this fluctuation. The present method of coping is to rely on overtime when demand is high and turning a blind eye to 'sickness' absence when things are slack. You have been told that the men like the overtime and the young married women like the 'sickness' absence, so it is quite a convenient arrangement.

Twenty-seven maintenance craftsmen and associated skilled personnel are all members of the AEU. The remaining shop floor employees are represented by the TGWU, although only 40–50 per cent are members. There have been seven stoppages in recent months due to breakdowns in negotiations about incentive payments. ACTS has begun recruiting members among white-collar staff, who have objected to plans for harmonization of terms and conditions between themselves and the shop-floor personnel.

14 Conflict resolution: Arbitration

Arbitration is resolving conflict between two parties by the judgement of a third. In negotiation we were examining an activity where the outcome depends on two parties finding an accommodation of their opposing points of view by their own efforts. In arbitration that initiative is passed to a single person or panel, recognized as independent by the participants, who 'hands down' a decision about the matter that the parties are obliged to accept.

There can be difficulties about the perceived independence of the arbitrator. If there is a disagreement between an employee and the supervisor, the employee may feel that a more senior manager arbitrating in the matter will inevitably be prone to favour the supervisor. It will, however, probably be the only avenue open to the employee, and the senior manager will at least be a different person from the one against whom the grievance lies. Also, the process of arbitration inevitably draws the arbitrator towards an impartial position.

Another difficulty can be the unwillingness of one party or other to accept the decision that has been made. No arbitration can be guaranteed sound before it takes place, so that dissatisfaction of one party or other is likely. Judicial systems typically provide the opportunity of appeal against a judgement, although only a small minority of cases ever go to appeal, but arbitration in industrial matters is less likely to provide that course. An important prerequisite is the willingness of the parties to seek arbitration in the first place. If it is a voluntary step by both, there is a commitment to accepting the judgement when it is made and it is difficult to reject it because it is unpalatable. The art of the arbitrator partly lies in avoiding a judgement which is a total agreement with the case of party A at the expense of party B or vice versa. There is usually scope for some reconciliation of the opposed positions. Not only does this reduce the degree of potential dissatisfaction with the outcome, it may also find a more mutually satisfying solution than the two parties could find unaided.

There is a limit, however, to the initiative that an arbitrator can take in proposing novel solutions, as the parties would be bound by proposals that might be unworkable. The arbitrator can never have enough detailed understanding of the working situation to impose new methods that can be guaranteed reliable in practice. That may be possible for the mediator or conciliator, who are also third parties trying to resolve conflict between two others, but their mode of operation is different. The mediator chairs discussions between opposed parties and helps agreement to be made around the table. The conciliator is the envoy who shuttles between the opposing camps trying to get them to understand the point of view of each other. In both those interventions the agreement is freely made by the parties. In arbitration the decision is made by the third party and imposed on the others; it must be workable, so the arbitrator must be cautious. The best-known form of arbitration in the field of employment is in the work of the Advisory, Conciliation and Arbitration Service (ACAS):

> If a dispute cannot be resolved by conciliation, ACAS may, at the request of one or more parties to the dispute, but subject to the consent of all of them, refer it for settlement to an independent arbitrator or arbitrators or to the Central Arbitration Committee (CAC). There is no legal compulsion on the parties to accept an arbitrator's award but, in practice, arbitrators' decisions are almost invariably accepted. (ACAS, 1980, p. 82)

Review topic 14.1

From your own experience, identify situations calling for arbitration, conciliation or mediation. Which of the three is required, and why?

Some industrial-relations agreements make provision for independent arbitration as the final step of an internal grievance procedure, and there are some examples of third-party intervention over a long period to 'facilitate problem-solving and negotiation in dispute areas' (Margerison and Leary, 1975, p. 3). Also there are many cases, day by day, where people in management posts have to 'sort out' feuds and squabbles between staff members. Mostly, these are brief, heated exchanges that erupt because two people cannot get on together, but sometimes a situation develops over a long period and a series of misunderstandings or more substantive problems have to be dealt with. All too frequently such matters are dismissed as 'failures of communication' or 'personality clashes', implying either that all that is necessary is more information or that resolution is not possible because the parties dislike each other. In fact, there are often useful possibilities for arbitration to improve working relationships by more thorough means than increasing information and despite people's likes and dislikes.

This chapter has something to say about all these varieties of arbitration.

The arbitration sequence

Preparation

(a) Arbitrator orientation

Arbitrating is not a commonplace activity, so the arbitrator may have to think through the situation beforehand and consider what the other participants will be expecting from the encounter. The disagreeing parties will look at the issue from two different frames of reference. This may be difficult for the arbitrator to remember, however obvious it sounds, in trying to establish some objective reality. Although the intervention of the arbitrator may induce modifications in the opening positions of the two parties, they will come to the encounter with with different values, priorities, hopes and fears.

The parties will also both be seeking justice in the sense that they are wanting to be proved right. They will seek confirmation of their actions by someone of higher status, not only to get their own way in a disagreement, but also to be able to claim justification for what they have done. In some serious disagreements the desire for justice may extend to wanting the other party to get their come-uppance, so one aspect of justice is to have oneself proved right and the other is for the opposing party to be proved wrong and, perhaps, to be punished in some way. A common example here is where a rank-and-file employee may want the supervisor not only proved wrong, but to apologize as well, knowing that the forced apology will be a humiliation.

If two parties go to arbitration the disagreement between them becomes a major issue. Not only will they be looking for justice being declared as on their side, they will also take with them a great fear of loss of face. The more firmly committed to a position you become, the more difficult it is to abandon, so that the arbitrator is faced with a difficult problem that has become more intractable by the arbitrator's involvement.

(b) Roles

There are at least three different roles in an arbitration encounter. The most important is that of the arbitrator. This is the term that will be used in this chapter, although the activities are sometimes very similar to those of the mediator.

On assuming office all British magistrates take an oath in which they swear to 'do right to all manner of people after the laws and usages of the realm without fear or favour, affection or ill-will.' That rather optimistic statement is the type of independence to which the arbitrator aspires. Unless the parties both believe that the matter will be viewed without prejudice to one side or the other, then there will be no confidence in the fairness of the outcome. This is not only independence from the two parties themselves, but also from extraneous influences such as government policy or sabre-rattling from an interested employer or trade union. It is unrealistic to expect any arbitrator to be immune to influence and devoid of prejudice, but some are seen to be more dispassionate than others. As well as independence, the arbitrator needs authority.

The nature of authority was briefly discussed in Chapter 10, and the authority of arbitrators will usually stem from their hierarchical position or from their wisdom. The extra quality they may possess is that aforementioned independence, which is not only a detachment from the immediate working situation but also the assumption of experience in other organizations of other problems. In judicial proceedings, in civil and other courts, the authority of the judge is shored up by a series of small methods: wearing a distinctive costume, sitting both apart from and above other participants in the proceedings, being addressed deferentially and requiring everyone else to stand when the judge enters or leaves the room. This is to emphasize the authority traditionally vested in the role. The arbitrator in an industrial dispute or office disagreement does not have all those trappings of authority, but is usually kept at a comfortable distance, both physically and socially, from other participants.

Review topic 14.2

Where you work, what 'trappings of authority' would be needed by someone attempting to arbitrate in a dispute?

The other two roles are those of complainant and respondent. They are so similar that the distinction is in many cases only theoretical, but there is a working assumption implied in those terms that one party is complaining about the action or inaction of someone else. It may be a union official complaining about the unacceptable new shift-working system that the management are proposing to introduce or the inadequate pattern of pay differentials. The idea of complainant/ respondent roles helps to provide a framework for running the encounter, especially in deciding who starts.

As with disciplinary encounters there is a small possibility of additional roles – either witnesses or advocates – but the essential structure is the triangle of arbitrator, complainant and respondent.

(c) Briefing
Before the encounter the arbitrator will need to review as much information about the matter as possible. This will vary from the one extreme of a hurried telephone conversation while two people fume outside the office, having just had a blazing row, to the other extreme where the arbitrator has detailed written statements of case from both parties beforehand, possibly embroidered by press comment or other background 'noise'.

(d) Objectives
The arbitrator will need to set up objectives for the meeting, even though these may not always be shared with the two parties. There will be process objectives and outcome objectives: the first will describe aspects of the relationship between the two parties that the arbitrator will be hoping to repair or develop during the discussion; the second will be the types of specific action which should be agreed before the end of the encounter. Some objectives will be derived from a reading of the papers or other preliminary information, depending upon what seems to be feasible and without prejudging the issue. There will be the more general objective of 'genuinely trying to search for a solution that is likely to be acceptable to both sides' (McCarthy and Ellis, 1973, p. 142) so that not only is there a resolution of the particular issue which is dividing the parties, but also the working relationship between them is at least partially repaired.

Linda Dickens (1979) provides a comment on the range of objectives available to third-party interventions in collective matters:

> It may be that the third party will seek to secure what he considers a 'just' or 'equitable' solution. On the other hand, he may take no interest in the form of the settlement – any settlement will do if the

parties agree to it, regardless of the merits of each side's position. This latter approach is the one which appears to characterize ACAS conciliation in such cases as unfair dismissal. The third party may look beyond the immediate dispute and attempt to lay the foundations for better relationships in the future. (Dickens, 1979, p. 302)

Encounter

(a) Setting

The setting of the encounter has to express the arbitrator's neutrality. This means ideally that it is not on the 'territory' of either the complainant or the respondent, unless there is a clear imbalance in power of the two parties at the outset, in which case a location favouring the weaker party might help to redress that imbalance and enhance the likelihood of a satisfactory outcome.

The formality of the setting will vary with the nature of the encounter, perhaps even the stage of the encounter. Walton (1969, p. 118) describes a mediated encounter between a personnel manager and a production superintendent that began in an office and later moved to a cocktail lounge and on again to a dining room:

> In the office setting there is a greater sense of urgency to get on with whatever one is doing. This is helpful in identifying many of the conflicting views and feelings in a short period of time. By shifting to the restaurant and by adding one round of drinks, the interaction could become somewhat more relaxed, allowing for a mixture of social banter and direct work on the relationship. This sort of mixture often facilitates the more integrative and educative work which must follow the identification and clarification of the issues. (Walton, 1969, p. 118)

In most cases the encounter will be fairly formal, even if it is only to enable the arbitrator to remain detached from the other participants, and the relative positioning of the arbitrator, complainant and respondent has to express this impartiality (Figure 14.1).

This mainly involves the arbitrator sitting at the apex of an imaginary triangle between the three of them. Mayerson (1979) even suggests that this neutrality has to be demonstrated in the way the arbitrator sits:

> Included in creating an atmosphere conducive to mediation are the facial expressions, posture and mannerisms of the mediator. Even the slightest hint of a tendency to lean in the direction of one side or

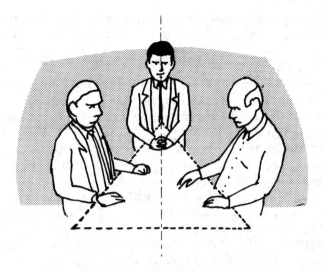

Figure 14.1 *The relative positioning of arbitrator,*
complainant and respondent expresses the impartiality of the
arbitrator

another may have an adverse effect on what the mediator is trying
to do. (Mayerson, 1979, p. 234)

(b) Opening

The proceedings can best begin with a statement by the arbitrator,
who is doing several things at this point. Firstly, the authority of the
arbitrator has to be set up. This is a prerequisite of effectiveness
anyway, as has already been seen, and that authority is now being
asserted, confirming the confidence of the parties in it and establishing control of the discussion that is to follow. The arbitrator also
demonstrates understanding of the issues, especially where submis-
sions have been provided beforehand.

The arbitrator sets the agenda at this stage. In the informal type of
arbitral setting the agenda will perhaps be little more than a
declaration that there are two sides to every argument and a
statement of who is to speak first. In more formal situations there will
be a specification of the sequence of events that is to come.

The arbitrator can try and set the tone for the proceedings by being
calm and measured in speech. At the outset the parties are likely to be
uneasy or angry and a calming tone from the arbitrator may facilitate
the opening exchanges. This is not to suggest that calmness is the
only appropriate atmosphere for all stages of the proceedings. At
some point it may be necessary for strength of feeling to be expressed

in order to provide that particular dimension, but at the opening calmness is helpful.

(c) The complaint

Having set the tone and taken control of the proceedings, the arbitrator can now proceed to ask for a statement from the complainant. Before the encounter begins it may be that one of the participants is clearly the complainant and will be the person to begin, but if that is not obvious then the arbitrator puts someone in that position by deciding who speaks first, with that particular advantage or disadvantage.

The complainant speaks fully, without interruption but with obvious attention from the arbitrator and silence (if necessary, imposed by the arbitrator) from the respondent. The possible intervention from the arbitrator is questioning to clarify or enlarge on some matter that may be obvious to the complainant, looking through that particular frame of reference, yet not clear to the arbitrator with less detailed knowledge. Clarification is mainly by direct questions either for information or for precision. An example of a direct question for information would be:

COMPLAINANT: This is the second time this has happened since Christmas.
ARBITRATOR: What happened last time?

Questioning for precision is usually needed when the complainant is not willing to make a clear statement, without which the complaint lacks substance:

COMPLAINANT: All my experience tells me that companies tend to take on commitments that are beyond their means.
ARBITRATOR: Are you saying that this company is taking on commitments that it has not the resources to handle?

When the statement of the complainant is complete the arbitrator will recapitulate what has been said in brief summary. This recapitulation improves or supports the communication between the parties and is similar to the technique of reflection. It is partly translating what has been said, where the complainant is reluctant to be precise or is not making complete sense, and partly it is to summarize and show understanding to the complainant. It is not a matter of turning at once to the respondent and saying, 'What he means . . . ' or 'What he is trying to say . . . ', as that is assuming the understanding without having confirmed it. The process of recapitulation is to the complainant, asking for confirmation, in the hearing of the respondent. The complainant can correct or add to the recapitulation by the arbitrator until there is an acceptable version. It is important that all these exchanges are with the impartial arbitrator rather than with the respondent, whose questions might be regarded as traps.

(d) The response

We now move to a similar statement, but from the respondent. This leaves out the stage, that is normal in legal proceedings, of cross-examination, wherein the respondent would ask questions of the complainant about what has been said. Even in relatively formal arbitrations this is not found: the move is directly to a response, which will include some refutation of what the complainant has alleged, some counter-charges and some failure to comment at all.

At the end of the response the arbitrator will again recapitulate, seeking the respondent's acceptance of this summary and taking up the points in the complaint that the respondent has ignored, so that they can either be accepted or refuted. Most of the difficulties will lie in the unanswered criticisms and in the counter-charges.

(e) Isolating issues

After the two opening statements the arbitrator will isolate the issues that divide the parties. There will already be some points of agreement that can be eliminated from further discussion but their existence is a part of the foundation of the rest of the encounter, as the parties will usually have found more common ground than they expected because they have now come together and stopped elaborating their dissatisfaction. However much still divides them, they will almost certainly have found some points of agreement that they did not expect. This is the basis on which they can now move forward, so some emphasis can usefully be given to those points, although it would be a foolish arbitrator who underestimated the significance of the differences that remained and who tried to smooth over real, outstanding difficulties.

The points of disagreement are what have to be tackled and they also have to be brought into focus, filtering out the irrelevances, platitudes and generalities so as to direct attention at what lies at the heart of the conflict, with complainant and respondent agreeing with the diagnosis. Until there is agreement on the agenda that is to follow, there is no way forward and the arbitrator's first interpretation may well not be shared by the participants, requiring the diagnosis to be reassessed and stated afresh until there is eventual agreement.

The arbitrator is not, of course, making any sort of right/wrong judgements between the participants unless the point is reached where one party or the other is declining acceptance of some particular point, despite the fact that the arbitrator has explored it and is satisfied that it is 'true'. In that case the arbitrator has no choice but to assert that this is the basis on which the matter has to proceed. This is a test of authority, but will only fail if the authority is too fragile anyway, or if the arbitrator is not genuinely being even-handed.

(f) Questioning

Now the arbitrator questions the parties about the points on which their stories diverge, so as both to face them with the contradictions and to produce a clearer idea in their minds of why they differ. The questions are phrased to direct attention to difficulties or obscurities without at any time impugning the integrity or objectives of the person being questioned. Questioning can switch quite quickly from complainant to respondent and back again to face them with the inconsistencies and perhaps enable them to see each other's point of view more clearly.

At some stage during this process there is the possibility that the problem will resolve itself. The parties will come to see the other point of view more clearly and may see their way through to a resolution without losing face. If this seems possible the arbitrator may encourage them to exchange directly with each other, abandoning the formality of the enforced triangular exchange. You need to be reasonably confident that this will succeed, because it is abandoning control.

If the matter is fully ventilated in as calm an atmosphere as possible, between antagonists of equally balanced power, settlement at this stage by this means is a likely outcome with the cold light of reason shone on the mistrust.

(g) Summing up

Although the matter may resolve itself at the questioning stage, it may be a more difficult issue needing a further contribution from the arbitrator, either because the parties lack confidence in their own ability to see the right answer or because one lacks trust in the other. In management–union encounters, for instance, union representatives may feel that they do not understand fully enough the technical aspects of proposed changes in a pay structure and would look to the arbitrator to provide that sort of expertise.

When acting as arbitrator you are now making a quite fresh contribution to the discussions, by introducing your own interpretation and some of your own suggestions about how the issue can be resolved or accommodated.

First of all, you will make comparisons between the two interpretations that have been presented during the encounter. This is largely a reiteration of what has been done earlier at the end of the complaint and the response in isolating issues, but it now comes at a different point of the proceedings and in the context of the two additional contributions you can now make: fresh alternatives and pacts. Because the complainant and respondent are so bound up with their own views, they can only see limited alternatives. As arbitrator, you are less hampered by personal involvement and will see possibilities that the others cannot, partly because of your detachment and partly because of the expertise you are able to impart into the discussion as a result of the knowledge you have of other situations. A pact is a particular form of alternative, whereby one party wants something of the other, and will only obtain it by providing something in exchange. Mayerson (1979, pp. 243–5) provides a neat example of this in her account of what she calls trade-offs. The arbitrator may, for example, suggest that a union claim that inspectors should receive a premium rate of pay, against management determination to maintain a uniform rate, might be considered more positively by the management if the number of inspectors could be agreed. The arbitrator moves with care in selecting pacts and other alternatives to propose, as the overriding objective is still trying to manoeuvre the parties into making their own agreement. Moving too far towards one party or the other makes that outcome less likely.

(h) Adjournment

In a complex case there will probably be one or more adjournments, as in negotiations, for everyone to reflect on their case while they are having a cup of tea and a rest, but there is a useful place for a 'tactical' adjournment after the arbitrator's summing up to allow time for the matter to be reassessed. Complainant and respondent will now see how the arbitrator's mind is working and will have some specific alternatives to consider. Things have moved a long way since the encounter began. There will be a new understanding and information, as well as – perhaps – new misunderstandings, so the parties are now working to a different scenario and have a better chance of making their own settlement. If they can manage that, it will be a much better arrangement than if they wait for the arbitrator to produce a solution, as they will be committing themselves voluntarily to an arrangement that they believe will work.

(i) Decision

The last resort is where the arbitrator tells the parties what to do. In unequivocal, yes/no problems this may be satisfactory, but in the typical wide-ranging, involved matters that only get to arbitration because they are so difficult, an externally imposed resolution can be inadequate. The arbitrator is, however, left with no choice. In the end a remedy has to be proposed, if the parties are unable or unwilling to find their own.

Follow-up

(a) Report

The report of the arbitrator will contain the judgement and the main parts of the summing up to explain and justify the decision that the arbitrator has made. Sometimes the decision is first conveyed to the parties in this way. The value of this document goes beyond simply saying what the decision is. It provides the parties with an objective statement about the matter. This will enable them to reflect on how the situation arose and how it might have been averted. It also provides a reference point for both sides in deciding whether the matter has later been resolved in the way that was laid down by the arbitrator.

Table 14.1 *The arbitration sequence*

Preparation
1. Review: orientation of parties.
2. Clarify: roles of:
   - arbitrator;
   - complainant;
   - respondent;
   - witnesses.
3. Decide: objectives for the encounter.

Encounter
1. Check: setting.
2. Develop the arbitration through the stages of:
   - opening;
   - the complaint;
   - the response;
   - isolating issues;
   - questioning;
   - summing up;
   - (perhaps) adjournment;
   - (if necessary) decision.

Follow-up
1. Report.
2. Recommendations.

(b) Recommendations

One of the aspects of the arbitrator's authority is that of walking away once the job is done. For this reason you may be asked to make general recommendations about matters surrounding the disputed question. Some arbitrators would feel that they can only do this if they make the recommendations to both parties rather than just to one; otherwise they would compromise the impartiality that was the basis of the decision they have offered.

References

ACAS (1980) *Industrial Relations Handbook*, HMSO, London.

Dickens, L. (1979) 'Conciliation, mediation and arbitration in Britain', in G. M. Stephenson and C. J. Brotherton (eds), *Industrial Relations: A social psychological approach*, John Wiley, Chichester.

Margerison, C. J. and M. Leary (1975) *Managing Industrial Conflicts*, MCB Books, Bradford.

Mayerson, E. N. (1979) *Shoptalk*, Saunders, Philadelphia.

McCarthy, W. E. J. and N. D. Ellis (1973) *Management by Agreement*, Hutchinson, London.

Walton, R. E. (1969) *Interpersonal Peacemaking*, Addison-Wesley, Reading, MA.

Exercise 14

Find a dispute in which you can try to mediate and act as honest broker between the disputing parties. This is not as easy as it sounds: firstly, because in some situations you may be practising with other people's deep feelings; and secondly, because in other situations you may be spoiling the fun of a good argument!

Notwithstanding the problems, keep an eye open for opportunities to try out the ideas in this chapter. It may be at work or in a social situation where your expressed interest is to understand what the row is about.

15 Three types of face-to-face interaction in groups

The classification used in this book does not include working in informal groups. There are a number of examples of this in the everyday life of organizations, so brief treatment of three types is provided in this concluding chapter.

Leading group discussion

Members of a discussion group both compete and co-operate. They will co-operate in the shared task of seeking understanding and developing answers, but they will also compete in wanting to appear shrewd, fluent and perceptive, especially if there are inequalities of status in the group. They will be even more anxious not to appear foolish. Members of the group will look to the leader for structure at the beginning: a strong indication of how to get started and assistance in developing the social interaction of the group process. As discussion unfolds the leader will become less obviously necessary to the group, but will still need to control the exchanges to ensure their effectiveness. This later control is the hardest part, as the voluble need to be reined in frequently and the diffident encouraged.

Small informal groups are being used more extensively in organizational life, especially since the introduction of team briefing, quality circles and similar attempts at employee involvement. This is due to the belief that some tasks are better undertaken by groups than by individuals. Blau and Scott (1963) list the main reasons for this view:

1. The sifting of suggestions in social interaction serves as an error-correction mechanism.
2. The social support furnished in interaction facilitates thinking.
3. The competition among members for respect mobilizes their energies for contributing to the task.

The apparent effectiveness in performance may, however, disappear when one considers the time that is involved: if one person can solve a problem in six hours it may be more cost-effective than five people solving the same problem in two. That criticism takes no account of either speed or implementation. If a matter is urgent, like correcting a fault in a spacecraft, a solution in two hours will be better than one in six, no matter how many people are involved. Also, it is one thing to solve a problem, but another to implement the solution. If those involved in putting a decision into practice take part in making the decision they will be better able to make it work, as there will be fewer queries for them to raise: they have been through the whole ratiocination needed already. Also they will be committed to success, on the grounds that people support that which they have helped to create.

Review topic 15.1

In your working experience, which of the following do you think are best dealt with by discussion in informal groups rather than by an individual taking executive action?

1. Deciding on disciplinary action about individuals.
2. Determining the points to be awarded to individual jobs in a job-evaluation exercise.
3. Negotiating with an overseas customer in the attempt to win an order for the first time.
4. Explaining changes in working practices.
5. Selecting individuals to be made redundant.
6. Selecting new office furniture.

In all informal groups the position of the leader is crucial, as it is not defined as clearly as in a committee. Much experimentation by social psychologists has been with leaderless groups, in that a leader has not been nominated at the outset, even though various group members make bids for leadership. In less rarefied activities there is usually a nominated leader, even if only by an assumption that the person with the greatest seniority or length of service will fill the role.

The size of the group will influence group effectiveness, according to the task. The larger the group the greater the problems of co-ordination. Most observers, and those experienced in leading groups, agree that five is the best number. Hare (1962) justified this on the grounds that an odd number of group members averted the possibility of deadlock, a single group member could be in a minority without the same pressure to conform with the majority that would exist in a smaller group, and there are enough people for members to shift roles easily. If the group task requires little co-ordination the size could increase, as may be needed for complex tasks, but for urgent matters there may be a case for reducing numbers.

The mix of group members may be heterogeneous or homogeneous. Heterogeneous composition is better for complex tasks requiring a diversity of opinion and expertise, and it is also preferred for creative tasks. Where accurate decision-making is important, there is again a preference for a heterogeneous composition, as the diversity of view will ensure a rigorous analysis. Homogeneous groups are better for sequential, interdependent tasks, as a chain is no stronger than its weakest link. Homogeneity is also preferred where the required level of co-operation is high or where the task is simple (Bass, 1965).

A common type of informal working group is the temporary taskforce, working party or project group, which comes into existence for a short time to tackle a single assignment before being disbanded. Group members are chosen for their particular expertise rather than their position in the organization, and their tasks are often to reduce costs or improve quality in one specific area of the operation. Management consultants depend heavily upon this mode of solving clients' problems. Du Brin comments:

> Interpersonal skills of a greater magnitude than most people possess may be required in the temporary task force arrangement. Rapport among strangers has to be built in a truncated period of time. Technically competent but interpersonally unsophisticated individuals fail because they require considerable time to establish trust and confidence with others. (du Brin, 1974, p. 204)

Every group leader needs to be able to assess the members of the group and work out how to mobilize their diverse competences and contributions to best effect. Here is a list of types of people and their distinctive contributions to group discussion (Figure 15.1). It is modelled on the work of Meredith Belbin.

- *The Shaper* influences discussion by developing thoughtful argument and following through particular topics that have been raised.

- *The Ideas Person* contributes novel suggestions and is likely to provide possibilities of breaking out of stalemate situations.

- *The Radical* believes that the group's task cannot be begun until something else has been completed – and the 'something else' is always beyond the group's control.

Figure 15.1 *The eight types of group member*

- *The Steady Eddy* is always cautious and aware of problems. This anxiety not to rock the boat can help a group avoid rashness, but a group comprised entirely of Steady Eddys would achieve little. They can be useful for taking the minutes.

- *The Team Worker* keeps the group going by joking when discussion gets too tense and always finding points on which to agree with other people.

- *The Monitor* likes to review progress and summarize what has been said. In many groups this is the main role of the leader, but a leader who is an enthusiast will need a monitor to keep track of what is happening.

- *The Shrinking Violet* has difficulty in getting in to the discussion and is intensely concerned not to sound foolish, requiring careful assistance – but not condescension – from the leader.

- *The Completer* likes to push things along, get things done and formulate conclusions.

Review topic 15.2

Take the above list and rewrite it in the ranked order that is most accurate as a description of your behaviour in meetings. Could you alter that ranking by changing your mode of participation? Do you want to? Why?

At the next meeting you attend, classify each participant in *one only* of the eight categories. Does the meeting need different people?

Making introductions

Do all members of the group know each other? With a close-knit team, like a senior-management group, introductions will obviously not be needed, but there may be a new member of the group, there may be members whose presence puzzles others (or themselves), and sometimes the group will be made up of relative strangers. The group leader has four basic strategies available for making sure that people know each other:

1. *Assume introductions are not needed*. The leader does not make any introductions, assuming them to be unnecessary.
2. *Introduce individuals*. The leader makes introductions 'from the chair', of those who are new to those who are established and vice versa, for example: 'I think we mostly know each other, but Chris is with

us for the first time, representing the systems-design group. Chris, on your right is Roger, from Customer Service, Sheila, from Distribution and Jan, who . . .'

3. *Ask people to introduce themselves.* 'Perhaps we could just go round the group, saying who we are and what our role is . . . . I'm Susan Danbury, from Central Finance. I've been asked to chair this group as I was one of the authors of the report which we have to discuss. On my right is . . . ?'

4. *Ask people to introduce others.* The leader asks pairs in the group to interview each other for five minutes and then introduce the person they have interviewed to everyone else. This method is particularly useful for a group of strangers, as it initiates discussion and eliminates the self-consciousness felt by many in saying 'I am . . . '

Introducing the meeting

The leader sets the scene by reminding everyone of why they have assembled and summarizing what it is they have to do. At this stage members of the group will welcome clear guidance and a suggested structure for the meeting, but the leader will need their consent by signing off with a comment like:

- 'Is that all right?'
- 'Is there anything I've missed, do you think?'

Introducing the discussion

The leader now opens the discussion by introducing the topic – or the first of several topics – for the group to develop. There are various ways of doing this:

1. *Setting out background information.* Adding to the initial introductory comments by providing more general information in a way that will focus the thinking of group members.

2. *Providing factual data.* Giving group members specific details about the initial topic and inviting their analysis.

3. *Offering an opinion.* Leading the group towards a conclusion by declaring your own beliefs first is a strong but risky opening. If you are articulating a view that most people will support, then the group will make quick progress. If there is likely to be dissent, then proceedings will be slowed down, as members of the group have to first grapple with the task of disagreeing with the leader, and then they have to sound out support for their own views.

4. *Asking a question.* Directing everyone's thinking by posing a question that opens up the topic. It is wise to move from the general to the particular, by setting up the initial discussion around the broader aspects of the question which can later be brought into much sharper focus.

Running the discussion

Although the leader will be less dominant as the discussion gets under way, there is still a need for control, and direction, using the following methods:

1. *Bringing people in.* The leader will need a balance of views, style and authority in the discussion. Without direction some group members will never speak and others will scarcely stop, but productive discussion will result from a blend of contributions form Shapers, Steady Eddys, Completers and so on. The leader will not only bring people in in a general way ('What do you think, Frank?') but will also shape the discussion by bringing people in for specific comment ('How does John's idea fit in with what you were saying earlier, Helen?').
2. *Shutting people up.* Curbing the voluble is difficult and can make everyone feel awkward if it is not well done, yet the discussion will not work if it is dominated by one or two people. Equally, the leader will fail if the voluble person is expressing a point of view for which there is broad support. In Chapter 3 there is a section about closing interviews which may be helpful, but other techniques for the leader are the following:

   - put one or two closed questions to a person in the middle of a diatribe;
   - give them a job to do ('Could you just jot down for us the main points of that, so that we can come back to it later?');
   - orientate them towards listening ('Can you see any problems with what Sheila wants to do?').

Focusing discussion

There is little need to sustain discussion on matters where everyone is agreed. Agreeing with each other is useful for social cohesion, but the leader needs regularly to direct discussion back to points of disagreement. It helps to bring in someone who has previously been neutral or silent on the matter and who may therefore have a different perspective.

Summarizing

Periodically the discussion will need to be summarized and a new direction introduced. Members of the group need to confirm the summary. This is usually a job for the lder, but there may be a monitor in the group to take it on.

Clarification

Occasionally someone in the group will make a contribution that others do not understand, so the leader will seek clarification, ensuring that the responsibility for the confusion is not on the person making the statement. 'Could you just go over that again, Fred' is better than 'I think what Fred is trying to say is . . . '

Closing the discussion

The leader will pick out from the discussion one or two workable hypotheses or points of general consensus and put them to the meeting for acceptance. Group members will look to the leader for that type of closure so that they have confirmation that their time has been well spent: only the leader can really see the wood for the trees. The best discussions finish on time!

Brainstorming

Brainstorming is a specialized technique first formulated in 1938 (Peel, 1988, p. 178) for developing a range of new ideas for examination:

> groups attempt to create a 'freewheeling' atmosphere where any ideas, however absurd, are recorded. Evaluation of the quality of ideas is strictly excluded and is carried out after the idea-generation phase is complete. [The] view is that the flow of ideas in the group will trigger off further ideas whereas the usual evaluative framework will tend to stifle imagination. This may be because group members are concerned not to appear ridiculous in the eyes of others. (Smith, 1973, p. 69)

Variations of this method are used in many areas of organizational life, where fresh ideas have to be found and creativity is required.

You need a flip chart, blackboard or overhead projector and someone who can write quickly and legibly. Before the meeting, decide what its purpose is. Is it one of the following:

- To find uses for a new idea.
- To generate a range of new ideas.
- To find a better way of doing something.
- To find a solution to a problem.

Running the meeting: Generating ideas

1. Appoint a note-taker.
2. Introduce the purpose of the meeting and ask group members to call out any idea relating to that purpose which comes into their heads.
3. Write ideas on a flip chart so that all members can see them.
4. Encourage members to develop the ideas of others ('hitch-hiking') as well as 'sparking' in different directions.
5. Ban judgement, as all ideas are valid, however bizarre, even if they seem to be repeating what has already been said. Even such subtle judgements as laughter, gasps of disbelief and nods of approval can inhibit or direct thinking. All should be banned at this stage.
6. Generate momentum, so that the group keeps going.
7. Reach a target number – say 65 – in 15 to 30 minutes.

Review topic 15.3

Try an informal brainstorm the next time you are on a car journey with one or two other people. Anyone will do: kids might even switch off their personal stereos in order to take part. Here are one or two possible starters:

1. Think of different uses for a piece of wood (e.g. 'Christmas dinner for woodworm').
2. What would make working life tolerable? (e.g. 'Voluntary euthanasia').
3. What is the greatest show on earth? (e.g. 'The House of Commons – when it's closed').

Running the meeting: Classifying the ideas

1. Collectively classify the ideas into five or six groups, possibly adding others suggested by the classification.
2. Ask the group to rank the ideas in each classification against questions such as:

- How new?
- How relevant?
- How feasible?

Committees

The committee is the standard form of decision-making in a bureaucracy or role culture. The form varies. The board of directors of a limited liability company is a committee, although the significance of each member's contribution may vary according to whether or not they combine board membership with a full-time post in the management of the company and the level of voting power they represent at a share-holders' meeting.

There are many safety committees, suggestions committees, consultative committees and other versions intended to reach collective decisions, even though individual members may have other concerns as well:

> Committees normally consist of 3–20 members . . . to varying degrees concerned about the task, which consists of solving problems and coming to decisions. They may stand to gain or lose personally; they may have their own ideas about the policy the committee should pursue, and may be committed to the success of the enterprise; they may be representatives of other bodies which elected them to the committee, and feel under obligation or pressure to defend their views. (Argyle, 1969, p. 53)

Committees operate in a formal way. There is invariably a chairman and normally minutes are kept. These may be drafted by a secretary during and after the meeting, with the draft then modified by the chairman, but eventually they have to be accepted by all members at the next meeting.

Although the chairman has considerable scope for determining the way in which proceedings are recorded and emphasized, there is less scope for determining decisions unless the committee members are remarkably compliant. Before a decision is reached it will be framed with some precision. It may be framed by the chairman in a leading way – 'Are we all agreed, then, that we proceed to seek tenders?' – or it may be put to the meeting as a motion from one of the members, seconded by another. In the latter case it will be worded precisely and the wording may be clarified or tidied up before the committee, as a whole, votes on it.

Other aspects of formality are that there is usually an agenda of items of business and some rules of procedure about who speaks, how voting is carried out, and the method of conducting debate by speaking 'through the chair' rather than to other committee members.

Committees are semi-permanent bodies, so that they tend to meet at predetermined times at regular intervals. This continuity makes important the issue of the terms of reference that the committee has: what it is intended to do, what range of authority it has, how it is to operate and how the membership is to be determined. The formality of committees gives the chairman considerable influence over proceedings as well as prescribing that authority in certain ways.

An early decision will be to settle the frequency of meetings. If the committee is to operate soundly its members have to learn to work together, even if that is not always the same as working harmoniously. Frequent meetings enable individual members to get to know each other's method of operating, and to establish working relationships and understandings, while practising their main job of functioning as a collective entity. In some cases there is a strong will towards co-operative working and even pride in belonging to the committee which is seen as doing a worthwhile job, although meetings have to be sufficiently frequent to continue the practice of working together, without having to rediscover it afresh every time. Some commentators believe that the cohesion of the committee's work depends upon the chairman enthusing each individual member:

> The chairman should take positive steps to ensure that each committee member believes his task to be worthwhile. Initially this may involve seeing individuals separately to discover what their attitudes are and to persuade them, if necessary, about the importance of the work. It may also entail personal discussions with individual members, outside committee work, to ascertain their current feelings and assure them of the value of their presence. (Sidney *et al.*, 1973, p. 112)

As with arbitration, the committee is dependent upon its chairman for its effectiveness, and chairmanship is in many ways similar to arbitrating, involving a degree of impartiality and acting as referee for the discussion that takes place. The first way in which the chairman exercises authority in the committee encounter itself is in introducing each agenda item, which will be presented to the committee from the chair with remarks that will influence the way in which committee members approach it. Phrases like, 'Perhaps we can just get this item out of the way' or 'I suppose this is the most important matter we have to consider this afternoon' will tend to make committee members treat those items in the same way. The chairman who assesses items in a way other committee members do not share will be challenged and committee proceedings may be protracted and made less effective.

Secondly, the chairman 'recognizes' people to contribute to the discussion. In trying to maintain a balance in the contributions some people will be called on to speak but not others. It is difficult to shut someone out entirely, but the discussion can be aided towards the achievement of a consensus or majority view by the sequence in which committee members speak. In most cases this is at random, but a chairman may call upon a bland, conciliatory member to speak at a time when the exchanges are getting overheated, or on a controversial, provocative member at a time when the discussion is losing its way and getting bogged down. This requires not only skill but also a shrewd knowledge of what the individual committee members can do. All through proceedings the chairman provides a sense of purpose, moving things along and keeping discussion to the point. This will include frequent raising of questions relating to the topic being reviewed in order to expand the committee's discussion of it. With each agenda item the chairman will summarize progress and conclusions, including agreement on what action is to be taken and by whom.

Helpful advice on committees is provided in books by Edgar Anstey (1965) and Malcolm Peel (1988). Andrew du Brin (1974, pp. 196–202) summarizes the disadvantages and advantages of committees, together with conditions favouring their use, which he regards as follows:

1. A committee will work effectively when it has the properties of an effective work group in general: optimum size and mix of membership, emotional support for all members, trust and confidence, and an appropriate system of rewards.
2. A chairman needs to be directive and task orientated in his behaviour, but not necessarily authoritarian.
3. A chairman will encourage constructive ideas if he shares power and collaborates with members.
4. Committee members should be technically and personally qualified to be members of the committee and be interested in serving on it.

In the end, committees produce decisions, even though some participants may feel that the process is a tedious and ineffective decision-making method. How can committee decisions be well founded and constructive? The following list is based on suggestions by Locke (1980, p. 167):

- *Legitimacy*. Committee members and other bodies accept the authority of the committee to make the decision, so that any opposition or disagreement will be based on the quality of the decision itself rather than the right of the committee to make it.

- *Action*. The decision should lead to some action, even if it is only settling an argument or agreeing to do nothing.

- *Soundness*. A decision should be taken only after hearing the best advice available and taking care that it fits both the facts of the current situation being considered and any relevant policies or precedents. Any decision which is a break with tradition should include an assessment of the implications of such a departure.

- *Feasibility*. It should be possible for the decision to be translated into action: there is no value in making a decision that is beyond the capability of the organization to implement.

- *Timing*. This is similar to the point made in discussing bargaining strategy. Decisions have to be taken at the time that is propitious. If there is no urgency there is no incentive to get to the bottom of the issue; if there is no time for discussion, the decision will be hasty and ill-informed. Also, some actions require decisions long before implementation.

Conclusion

A large part of the contemporary management role is maintaining an effective system of interpersonal relationships so as to integrate the diverse activities of those working in the organization, focusing their efforts towards common goals. Although organizational structures play a large part in this process, the manager's ability to handle a range of interactive episodes with a variety of other people is the key factor in communicative success. This requires from managers not only greater understanding and the development of personal effect-iveness: it also requires action.

Implicit in the managerial role as boundary spanner or liaison is the need to transcend structural barriers that impede the flow of communication in an organization. The manager who does not or cannot maintain an effective network of interpersonal communication relationships will become a victim of executive isolation. To avoid isolation, managers must take the initiative in establishing direct communication with their subordinates. Walking out into work areas and inviting employees into the manager's office are more likely to generate effective communication than a traditional open-door policy, which requires the subordinate to take the first step. (Baskin and Aronoff, 1980, p. 160)

The material of this book does not relate only to interactive 'set pieces' but to all the communications activity of organizational life, each incident of which will follow one or more of the patterns described. Managers need not only to respond, but also to initiate.

The final comment is to remind everyone that style without substance is dangerous. This can be illustrated by a literary allusion. Hamlet's uncle, the King, is so full of anguish about his brother's murder ('O my offence is rank, it smells to Heaven') that he seeks to expiate his guilt in prayer but has to abandon the attempt because his heart is not in it:

> My words fly up, my thoughts remain below.
> Words without thoughts never to Heaven go.

The most carefully orchestrated speech or painstaking counselling interview is unsuccessful if it is mere words. We need not only words, and a way with words, but also thoughts which match the words and are right for the situation in which they are uttered.

Let us finish with another anecdote. A company was introducing a pension scheme with a condition that all employees should join. The only person who would not take part was Fred, who had been there since time immemorial. The personnel manager, works convenor and works director all failed to persuade Fred to change his mind. The company chairman heard of the problem and called Fred into his office:

CHAIRMAN: 'Fred, sign here or you're fired.'

FRED: 'Yes sir, right away, sir.'

CHAIRMAN: 'If you sign so readily when I ask you, why didn't you sign before?'

FRED: 'Ah well, no-one else explained it properly.'

References

Anstey, E. (1965) *Committees: How they work and how to work them*, Allen & Unwin, London.

Anstey, E., C. A. Fletcher, and J. Walker, (1976) *Staff Appraisal and Development*, Allen & Unwin, London.

Argyle, M. (1969) *Social Interaction*, Tavistock Publications, London.

Bales, R. F. (1950) *Interaction Process Analysis*, Addison-Wesley, Cambridge, MA.

Bales, R. F. (1958) 'Task roles and social roles in problem-solving groups', in E. E. Maccoby, T. Newcomb and E. L. Hartley (eds), *Readings in Social Psychology*, Holt, Rinehart & Winston, New York.

Baskin, A. W. and C. E. Aronoff (1980) *Interpersonal Communication in Organizations*, Goodyear, Santa Monica, CA.

Bass, B. M. (1965) *Organisation Psychology*, Allyn & Bacon, Boston.

Blau, P. M. and W. R. Scott (1976) 'Processes of communication in formal organizations' (1963), in M. Argyle, (ed.), *Social Encounters*, Penguin, Harmondsorth.

du Brin, A. J. (1974) *Fundamentals of Organizational Behavior*, Pergamon Press, New York.

Hare, P. A. (1962) *Handbook of Small Group Research*, Free Press, New York.

Locke, M. (1980) *How to Run Committees and Meetings*, Macmillan, London.

Maier, N. R. F. (1958) *The Appraisal Interview*, Wiley, New York.

Peel, M. (1988) *How To Make Meetings Work*, Kogan Page, London.

Randell, G., R. Shaw, P. Packard and J. Slater (1972) *Staff Appraisal*, Institute of Personnel Management, London.

Sidney, E., M. Brown and M. Argyle (1973) *Skills with People*, Hutchinson, London.

Smith, P. B. (1973) *Groups within Organizations*, Harper & Row, London.

Index